RAMSES THE GREAT

◆ ◆ ◆

❖ ANCIENT WORLD LEADERS ❖

ALEXANDER THE GREAT

ATTILA THE HUN

CHARLEMAGNE

CLEOPATRA

CYRUS THE GREAT

DARIUS THE GREAT

GENGHIS KHAN

HAMMURABI

HANNIBAL

JULIUS CAESAR

KING DAVID

NEFERTITI

QUEEN OF SHEBA

RAMSES THE GREAT

SALADIN

XERXES

RAMSES THE GREAT

SILVIA ANNE SHEAFER

CHELSEA HOUSE
PUBLISHERS
An imprint of Infobase Publishing

Frontispiece: Head of a colossal statue of Pharaoh Ramses II. Facade of the Great Temple at Abu Simbel, Egypt.

Ramses the Great
Copyright © 2009 by Infobase Publishing

Chelsea House
An imprint of Infobase Publishing
132 West 31st Street
New York, NY 10001

Library of Congress Cataloging-in-Publication Data

Sheafer, Silvia Anne.
 Ramses the Great / Silvia Anne Sheafer.
   p. cm. — (Ancient world leaders)
 Includes bibliographical references and index.
 ISBN 978-0-7910-9637-6 (hardcover)
 1. Ramses II, King of Egypt—Juvenile literature. 2. Egypt—History—Nineteenth dynasty,
ca. 1320–1200 B.C.—Juvenile literature. 3. Pharaohs—Biography—Juvenile literature. I. Title.
II. Series.
 DT88.S54 2008
 932'.014092—dc22
 [B]   2008004871

Chelsea House books are available at special discounts when purchased in bulk quantities for businesses, associations, institutions, or sales promotions. Please call our Special Sales Department in New York at (212) 967-8800 or (800) 322-8755.

You can find Chelsea House on the World Wide Web at http://www.chelseahouse.com

Text design by Lina Farinella
Cover design by Jooyoung An

Printed in the United States of America

Bang NMSG 10 9 8 7 6 5 4 3 2 1

This book is printed on acid-free paper.

All links and Web addresses were checked and verified to be correct at the time of publication. Because of the dynamic nature of the Web, some addresses and links may have changed since publication and may no longer be valid.

CONTENTS

Foreword: On Leadership 6
Arthur M. Schlesinger, Jr.

1 Young Ramses II 12

2 Sixty-seven Kings 23

3 Ramses Crowned King of Egypt 35

4 Daily Life in Ancient Egypt 46

5 Master Builder 58

6 Master Strategist 71

7 Fields of Endeavor 82

8 The Peace Treaty 91

9 Nightfall 100

10 Egypt Thereafter 110

Chronology 119
Bibliography 121
Further Reading 124
Photo Credits 125
Index 126
About the Authors 131

Arthur M. Schlesinger, Jr.
On Leadership

L eadership, it may be said, is really what makes the world go round. Love no doubt smoothes the passage; but love is a private transaction between consenting adults. Leadership is a public transaction with history. The idea of leadership affirms the capacity of individuals to move, inspire, and mobilize masses of people so that they act together in pursuit of an end. Sometimes leadership serves good purposes, sometimes bad; but whether the end is benign or evil, great leaders are those men and women who leave their personal stamp on history.

Now, the very concept of leadership implies the proposition that individuals can make a difference. This proposition has never been universally accepted. From classical times to the present day, eminent thinkers have regarded individuals as no more than the agents and pawns of larger forces, whether the gods and goddesses of the ancient world or, in the modern era, race, class, nation, the dialectic, the will of the people, the spirit of the times, history itself. Against such forces, the individual dwindles into insignificance.

So contends the thesis of historical determinism. Tolstoy's great novel *War and Peace* offers a famous statement of the case. Why, Tolstoy asked, did millions of men in the Napoleonic Wars, denying their human feelings and their common sense, move back and forth across Europe slaughtering their fellows? "The war," Tolstoy answered, "was bound to happen simply because it was bound to happen." All prior history determined it. As for leaders, they, Tolstoy said, "are but the labels that serve to give a name to an end and, like labels, they have the least possible connection with the event." The greater the leader, "the more conspicuous the inevitability and the predestination of every act he commits." The leader, said Tolstoy, is "the slave of history."

Determinism takes many forms. Marxism is the determinism of class. Nazism the determinism of race. But the idea of men and women as the slaves of history runs athwart the deepest human instincts. Rigid determinism abolishes the idea of human freedom—the assumption of free choice that underlies every move we make, every word we speak, every thought we think. It abolishes the idea of human responsibility, since it is manifestly unfair to reward or punish people for actions that are by definition beyond their control. No one can live consistently by any deterministic creed. The Marxist states prove this themselves by their extreme susceptibility to the cult of leadership.

More than that, history refutes the idea that individuals make no difference. In December 1931 a British politician crossing Fifth Avenue in New York City between 76th and 77th Streets around 10:30 p.m. looked in the wrong direction and was knocked down by an automobile— a moment, he later recalled, of a man aghast, a world aglare: "I do not understand why I was not broken like an eggshell or squashed like a gooseberry." Fourteen months later an American politician, sitting in an open car in Miami, Florida, was fired on by an assassin; the man beside him was hit. Those who believe that individuals make no difference to history might well ponder whether the next two decades would have been the same had Mario Constasino's car killed Winston Churchill in 1931 and Giuseppe Zangara's bullet killed Franklin Roosevelt in 1933. Suppose, in addition, that Lenin had died of typhus in Siberia in 1895 and that Hitler had been killed on the western front in 1916. What would the 20th century have looked like now?

For better or for worse, individuals do make a difference. "The notion that a people can run itself and its affairs anonymously," wrote the philosopher William James, "is now well known to be the silliest of absurdities. Mankind does nothing save through initiatives on the part of inventors, great or small, and imitation by the rest of us—these are the sole factors in human progress. Individuals of genius show the way, and set the patterns, which common people then adopt and follow."

Leadership, James suggests, means leadership in thought as well as in action. In the long run, leaders in thought may well make the greater difference to the world. "The ideas of economists and political philosophers, both when they are right and when they are wrong," wrote John Maynard Keynes, "are more powerful than is commonly understood. Indeed the world is ruled by little else. Practical men, who believe themselves to be quite exempt from any intellectual influences, are usually the slaves of some defunct economist. . . . The power of vested interests is vastly exaggerated compared with the gradual encroachment of ideas."

But, as Woodrow Wilson once said, "Those only are leaders of men, in the general eye, who lead in action. . . . It is at their hands that new thought gets its translation into the crude language of deeds." Leaders in thought often invent in solitude and obscurity, leaving to later generations the tasks of imitation. Leaders in action—the leaders portrayed in this series—have to be effective in their own time.

And they cannot be effective by themselves. They must act in response to the rhythms of their age. Their genius must be adapted, in a phrase from William James, "to the receptivities of the moment." Leaders are useless without followers. "There goes the mob," said the French politician, hearing a clamor in the streets. "I am their leader. I must follow them." Great leaders turn the inchoate emotions of the mob to purposes of their own. They seize on the opportunities of their time, the hopes, fears, frustrations, crises, potentialities. They succeed when events have prepared the way for them, when the community is awaiting to be aroused, when they can provide the clarifying and organizing ideas. Leadership completes the circuit between the individual and the mass and thereby alters history.

It may alter history for better or for worse. Leaders have been responsible for the most extravagant follies and most monstrous crimes that have beset suffering humanity. They have also been vital in such gains as humanity has made in individual freedom, religious and racial tolerance, social justice, and respect for human rights.

There is no sure way to tell in advance who is going to lead for good and who for evil. But a glance at the gallery of men and women in ANCIENT WORLD LEADERS suggests some useful tests.

One test is this: Do leaders lead by force or by persuasion? By command or by consent? Through most of history leadership was exercised by the divine right of authority. The duty of followers was to defer and to obey. "Theirs not to reason why/ Theirs but to do and die." On occasion, as with the so-called enlightened despots of the 18th century in Europe, absolutist leadership was animated by humane purposes. More often, absolutism nourished the passion for domination, land, gold, and conquest and resulted in tyranny.

The great revolution of modern times has been the revolution of equality. "Perhaps no form of government," wrote the British historian James Bryce in his study of the United States, *The American Commonwealth*, "needs great leaders so much as democracy." The idea that all people should be equal in their legal condition has undermined the old structure of authority, hierarchy, and deference. The revolution of equality has had two contrary effects on the nature of leadership. For equality, as Alexis de Tocqueville pointed out in his great study *Democracy in America*, might mean equality in servitude as well as equality in freedom.

"I know of only two methods of establishing equality in the political world," Tocqueville wrote. "Rights must be given to every citizen, or none at all to anyone . . . save one, who is the master of all." There was no middle ground "between the sovereignty of all and the absolute power of one man." In his astonishing prediction of 20th-century totalitarian dictatorship, Tocqueville explained how the revolution of equality could lead to the *Führerprinzip* and more terrible absolutism than the world had ever known.

But when rights are given to every citizen and the sovereignty of all is established, the problem of leadership takes a new form, becomes more exacting than ever before. It is easy to issue commands and enforce them by the rope and the stake, the concentration camp and the *gulag*. It is much harder to use argument and achievement to overcome opposition and win consent. The Founding Fathers of the United States understood the difficulty. They believed that history had given them the opportunity to decide, as Alexander Hamilton wrote in the first Federalist Paper, whether men are indeed capable of basing government on "reflection and choice, or whether they are forever destined to depend . . . on accident and force."

Government by reflection and choice called for a new style of leadership and a new quality of followership. It required leaders to be responsive to popular concerns, and it required followers to be active and informed participants in the process. Democracy does not eliminate emotion from politics; sometimes it fosters demagoguery; but it is confident that, as the greatest of democratic leaders put it, you cannot fool all of the people all of the time. It measures leadership by results and retires those who overreach or falter or fail.

It is true that in the long run despots are measured by results too. But they can postpone the day of judgment, sometimes indefinitely, and in the meantime they can do infinite harm. It is also true that democracy is no guarantee of virtue and intelligence in government, for the voice of the people is not necessarily the voice of God. But democracy, by assuring the right of opposition, offers built-in resistance to the evils inherent in absolutism. As the theologian Reinhold Niebuhr summed it up, "Man's capacity for justice makes democracy possible, but man's inclination to justice makes democracy necessary."

A second test for leadership is the end for which power is sought. When leaders have as their goal the supremacy of a master race or the promotion of totalitarian revolution or the acquisition and exploitation of colonies or the protection of greed and privilege or the preservation of personal power, it is likely that their leadership will do little to advance the cause of humanity. When their goal is the abolition of slavery, the liberation of women, the enlargement of opportunity for the poor and powerless, the extension of equal rights to racial minorities, the defense of the freedoms of expression and opposition, it is likely that their leadership will increase the sum of human liberty and welfare.

Leaders have done great harm to the world. They have also conferred great benefits. You will find both sorts in this series. Even "good" leaders must be regarded with a certain wariness. Leaders are not demigods; they put on their trousers one leg after another just like ordinary mortals. No leader is infallible, and every leader needs to be reminded of this at regular intervals. Irreverence irritates leaders but is their salvation. Unquestioning submission corrupts leaders and demeans followers. Making a cult of a leader is always a mistake. Fortunately, hero worship generates its own antidote. "Every hero," said Emerson, "becomes a bore at last."

The signal benefit the great leaders confer is to embolden the rest of us to live according to our own best selves, to be active, insistent, and resolute in affirming our own sense of things. For great leaders attest to the reality of human freedom against the supposed inevitabilities of history. And they attest to the wisdom and power that may lie within the most unlikely of us, which is why Abraham Lincoln remains the supreme example of great leadership. A great leader, said Emerson, exhibits new possibilities to all humanity. "We feed on genius. . . . Great men exist that there may be greater men."

Great leaders, in short, justify themselves by emancipating and empowering their followers. So humanity struggles to master its destiny, remembering with Alexis de Tocqueville: "It is true that around every man a fatal circle is traced beyond which he cannot pass; but within the wide verge of that circle he is powerful and free; as it is with man, so with communities." ◆

1

Young
Ramses II

EGYPT'S GOLDEN SUNLIGHT LIT THE OPEN-AIR CLASSROOM WHERE fourteen-year-old Prince Ramses studied. Dressed in a short cloth kilt, his reddish hair was brushed over one ear in the traditional hair lock style. Admission to the royal academy of Ka, "the closed protected, nourishing place," was considered a prize. Like other royal children destined for high government positions, Ramses was taken from the palace as a child and provided with a guardian and tutor. At age 10 he was given the honorary title of commander in chief of the Egyptian army.

Pharaoh Sethos I, his father, governed the flourishing Egyptian kingdom and battled Hittite insurgents from the empire of Anatolia (now the country of Turkey) or minor warlords who stirred up trouble in his Asian and Syro-Palestinian territories.

Queen Tuya, Ramses' refined and beautiful mother, reigned as the great royal wife with numerous responsibilities. She ruled over the court harem, granted audiences to provincial leaders, and demonstrated concern for the welfare of her people. When the pharaoh (king) was absent, she oversaw matters of the royal court. Though it was whispered in palace gossip that she favored her younger son—his older brother had died—she did not encourage familiarity, and Ramses did not seek her confidence. She adored both Ramses and his sister Tia, and their frequent meetings were usually on a social level, such as lunch in her royal garden. Ramses' confidants were personal friends from the academy.

Ramses had been a pampered prince who taunted priests with adolescent pranks, yet he excelled in drawing delicate and beautiful hieroglyphs and calculating a pyramid slope to the nearest degree. His rigorous education included mathematics, science, chemistry, and literature. He also was challenged by demanding athletic skills to become an expert sportsman and possible future charioteer. Muscularly built and ambitious, he excelled in competitive games such as archery, horsemanship, and swimming.

The day arrived when Pharaoh Sethos came for young Ramses. Without explanation, he took his son from his hieroglyph class. Cautious yet respectful of the king, the father he'd never really known, Ramses was quietly curious about their ride into the countryside. The king's two-horse chariot paused as it approached a desolate marsh of reeds and rushes, a dark haven for venomous snakes, wild animals, and scattered birds. Among the tall papyrus, Ramses spotted a bull. When the male beast caught sight of the young prince, it snorted and pawed at the earth. Ancient Egyptian legend portrayed the bull as a celestial animal that lived in the underworld and burned with brilliant orange fire. Ramses stared at the bull, tense and uncertain. Then he turned questioningly toward his father. What was he to do?

As if to question the boy's bravery, the pharaoh glared at his son. Now, Ramses understood. He had been brought into the

This limestone relief from the Nineteenth Dynasty depicts Ramses II as a child. In ancient Egypt, it was fashionable for young boys to shave their heads clean, save for a braided side lock. As with other boys of the time, when Ramses II became a man, his side lock was cut off.

soggy thickets to face the bull; it was a test of his courage! If he was ever to become a pharaoh, or even an active warrior in his father's army, he must prove himself brave and unafraid.

Ramses was strong. He'd excelled in combative athletics at school and knew fortitude must equal physical strength. But could he tackle a wild, angry bull?

Impatient with the young intruder, the beast snorted and squared its horns.

King Sethos tossed Ramses a lasso. The boy twirled the rope and swung its loop toward the bull's horns. He missed and fell flat on his back.

Enraged by its failed kill, the bull clawed at the reeds and stubbornly lowered its horns. With his feet firmly dug into the wet earth, Ramses frowned at the burning eyes of the beast. He must kill the bull or die trying!

With a mighty kick of its rear legs, the animal lurched with such violence that the grass seemed to explode. Seconds before his horns dug into Ramses' flesh, the pharaoh grabbed the rope and lassoed the bull. The earth rumbled as Sethos tossed the enraged animal to the ground. Swiftly he pulled a dagger from his belt and demanded Ramses cut off the tail of the very much alive bull.

There in the marsh was his first test. Prince Ramses had conquered his fear. The pharaoh quickly retrieved his blade and cut off Ramses' hair lock. His youth had ended.

RAMSES' LEGACY BEGINS

Ramses II's prominent roll as a great leader of ancient history was forged the day he was born, about 3,200 years ago. He was crowned pharaoh of Egypt in 1279 B.C., when he was 22 years old. Tall for an Egyptian, he was handsome, slim, and athletic, and he looked every inch a god king. Soon after his coronation, he prepared to reconquer Egypt's vast empire. His future was stamped and sealed. His reign lasted more than 67 years, longer than almost any other pharaoh.

Ramses II is recognized for his military leadership, for his peacekeeping abilities, and for the colossal monuments he left behind. He built the largest freestanding statue of himself—60 feet high (18.28 meters)—before it toppled in antiquity. He also built one of Egypt's most famous temples, Abu Simbel. Egyptian scholar and archaeologist Peter Clayton wrote that the results were remarkable. "As a monument builder Ramses II stands pre-eminent amongst the pharaohs of Egypt. Although

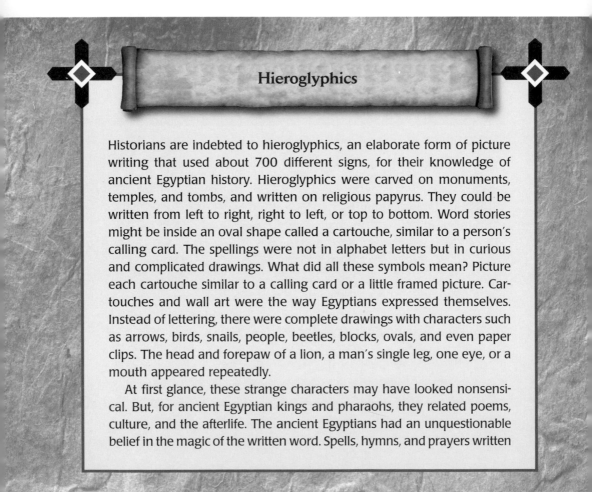

Hieroglyphics

Historians are indebted to hieroglyphics, an elaborate form of picture writing that used about 700 different signs, for their knowledge of ancient Egyptian history. Hieroglyphics were carved on monuments, temples, and tombs, and written on religious papyrus. They could be written from left to right, right to left, or top to bottom. Word stories might be inside an oval shape called a cartouche, similar to a person's calling card. The spellings were not in alphabet letters but in curious and complicated drawings. What did all these symbols mean? Picture each cartouche similar to a calling card or a little framed picture. Cartouches and wall art were the way Egyptians expressed themselves. Instead of lettering, there were complete drawings with characters such as arrows, birds, snails, people, beetles, blocks, ovals, and even paper clips. The head and forepaw of a lion, a man's single leg, one eye, or a mouth appeared repeatedly.

At first glance, these strange characters may have looked nonsensical. But, for ancient Egyptian kings and pharaohs, they related poems, culture, and the afterlife. The ancient Egyptians had an unquestionable belief in the magic of the written word. Spells, hymns, and prayers written

Khufu created the Great Pyramid, Ramses' hand lay over the whole land. . . . His genuine building achievements are on a Herculean scale," Clayton said in Jim Whiting's *The Life and Times of Rameses the Great*.

Ramses lived in big ways. He had seven royal wives, numerous secondary wives and concubines, and nearly 100 royal children who energized his palace. Egyptian scholars disagree on the exact numbers, although ancient hieroglyphics reveal a large family. Abdel Halim Nur el-Din, head of the department of Egyptology at Cairo University said, "Ramses was a great

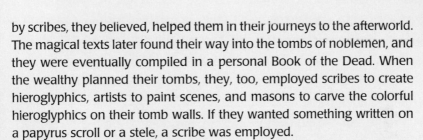

by scribes, they believed, helped them in their journeys to the afterworld. The magical texts later found their way into the tombs of noblemen, and they were eventually compiled in a personal Book of the Dead. When the wealthy planned their tombs, they, too, employed scribes to create hieroglyphics, artists to paint scenes, and masons to carve the colorful hieroglyphics on their tomb walls. If they wanted something written on a papyrus scroll or a stele, a scribe was employed.

The ancient Egyptian alphabet had 24 letters, all consonants. Vowel sounds were not written. Sometimes the words would be a single character or a whole syllable, and could not be pronounced. The writings were called "words of the gods" because they believed that Thoth, the god of learning, invented spelling. The word "hieroglyph" was first used in 300 B.C. after the Greeks came to Egypt and saw the characters carved on the temple walls. In the Greek language, *hiero* means "holy" and *glyph* means "writing." For nearly 3,000 years, no one understood what these pictures meant or how they sounded. Sometimes, by accident, riddles can be solved. Such happened with the discovery of the Rosetta Stone.

military man, he was a man of peace, he was the greatest builder in ancient Egypt, he had the biggest statue, he was the husband of a well-known lady, he had more children than any king of Egypt, he lived nearly longer than any king of Egypt, even now he has the best-preserved mummy. The largest square in Egypt is called Ramses, the biggest street in Egypt is called Ramses. . . . In ancient and modern times, there is no doubt that Ramses II is great."

Ramses' extraordinary popularity and power surpassed all other pharaohs and left an ineradicable mark on ancient Near Eastern history. He was a famous warrior who rode gloriously into battle with a tame lion at his side. He slew thousands of enemies as his campaigns ensued. The Qadesh conflict was one of the most heroic battles in Egyptian history. It lasted four days. Badly outnumbered, Ramses was losing the battle. Almost single-handedly, he and his few soldiers fought back until reinforcements arrived, turning defeat into victory. Though his military exploits had mixed results, he was the first king in world history to sign a peace treaty with the enemy, the Hittite Empire. The treaty ended long years of brutal fighting and insurgent hostilities between the Hittites, Libyans, and Nubians. It is considered a masterful accomplishment forged between two war-embedded countries.

Historian Dr. Robert A. Guisepi commented on the treaty on the International World History Project Web site: "Its strikingly modern character is revealed in clauses providing for nonaggression, mutual assistance, and extradition of fugitives."

LIFE IN ANCIENT MEMPHIS

Memphis, the ancient capital of Lower Egypt, once stood on the fertile west bank of the Nile Delta. Menes of Tanis founded the city in about 3100 B.C. To secure the city from seasonal Nile flooding, he built a complex system of dikes and canals for protection and as a symbolic entity—"the white wall"—around the city. Memphis reached its peak of prestige as administrative and religious center during the Sixth Dynasty. It was believed to be the largest city in the world. It was here that Ramses II, son of King Sethos and Queen Tuya, first rode beside his father and engraved his lasting legacy.

Stone towers, colorful domes, obelisks as tall as oil derricks, and graceful swans and swooping pelicans enriched the Memphis landscape. There were great universities and bustling jewelry shops laden with gold, turquoise, and lapis lazuli. Politics and gossip were discussed over beer and wine in cool, shaded recesses. Date palms, sycamores, and acacia trees shadowed verdant parks adorned with gigantic pink granite statues. Sweet-smelling lotus scented reflecting ponds and tantalized the fish. The cult of Ptah, god of artists, had a glorious stone temple, as did that of the god Apis, the sacred bull. Nearby was the Saqqara, a necropolis for royalty, minor burials, and cult ceremonies—the oldest complete hewn-stone complex known in world history.

Pharaohs, such as King Sethos, and wealthy nobles lived in magnificent palaces or sumptuous villas with spacious courtyards and gardens of fruit trees and flowers. They dined on alabaster dinnerware and drank from exquisitely designed faience cups served by scores of servants. Lesser Egyptians and the poor lived in mud houses. Hippopotamuses and crocodiles tangled fishing lines in the Delta canals.

Scholarly writers have connected Ramses II with Moses. According to the Bible, Memphis was called Moph or Noph. Taking this a step further, it was the seat of the pharaoh in the time of Joseph of Nazareth, foster father of Jesus. Some historians believe that Ramses II was the pharaoh of the Exodus and place him as befriending Moses.

WISDOM AND HARMONY

Ramses studied the law of Maat, the lovely goddess of truth, balance, and order. He sought to understand the concepts of Egyptian wisdom and to place them in relationship to his own life. Maat set 42 declarations of purity, laws that expressed a ubiquitous concept of right from wrong. It was somewhat like the underlying concepts of Taoism and Confucianism. Many of the concepts were classified into laws. They were discussed by philosophers and officials who referred to the spiritual text as the Book of the Dead. Egyptians believed the universe was above everything else. It functioned with predictability, the cycles of the universe always remained constant, and in the moral sphere, purity was rewarded and sin was punished. Morally and physically, the universe was in perfect balance. It was thought that if Maat didn't exist, the universe would become chaos!

Another set of philosophical ideas inspired Ramses' thinking. Vizier Ptahhotep's Maxims, conceived about 2200 B.C., were instructions in good discourse for young men of influential families soon to assume prominent civil offices. Its final precept instructed, "Do that which your master bids you. Twice good is the precept of his father, from whom he has issued, from his flesh. What he tells us let it be fixed in your heart; to satisfy him greatly let us do for him more than he has prescribed. Verily a good son is one of the gifts of Ptah, a son who does even better than he has been told to do. For his master he does what is satisfactory, putting himself with all his heart on the part of right. So I shall bring it about that your body shall be healthful, that the Pharaoh shall be satisfied with you in all circumstance and that you shall obtain years of life without default. It has caused me on earth to obtain one hundred and ten years of life, along with the gift of the favor of the Pharaoh among the first of those whom their works have ennobled, satisfying the Pharaoh in a place of dignity," explained Charles F. Horne in *The Sacred Books and Early Literature of the East.*

Because Ramses' older brother was in line for the throne, Ramses believed he'd be granted a high government position rather than become pharaoh. As such, he understood the future of his royal station and prepared for the eventuality.

This detail from the Temple of Ramses II illustrates the pharaoh at the Battle of Qadesh. The battle was a turning point for the young and inexperienced ruler: It was there that Ramses proved himself capable of expanding and protecting his kingdom.

In time, Ramses faced more mental and physical challenges conceived by Pharaoh Sethos: surviving the desert's burning heat during the day and the cold of night; handling poisonous creatures that slithered in the reeds and sunned themselves by day; navigating the swamps and the unpredictable twists and currents of the Delta canals; gauging the winds and stars for navigational direction. He labored in stone quarries, learning the trade of stonecutters, and honed his hunting skills. With each test the young prince proved himself equal to the task, proof that he was worthy of his royal birthright and the respect of his father.

He began to appreciate that truth and justice, exampled by his father, were what held Egypt together. Ramses' heightened awareness of his royal position and commanding interest in all Egyptian matters led to his extraordinary place in Near Eastern history. Ramses had the genius, character, and defined sensibilities to empower his people to engage in massive construction projects and wage bitter wars that ultimately led to years of prosperity and peace. Ramses the Great's rise to dominance and leadership provides a comprehensive overview of ancient world history.

2

Sixty-seven Kings

IN A SHALLOW GRAVE ON THE EDGE OF THE EGYPTIAN DESERT, CURLED up on its side, lay a skeleton. Its brittle brown bones rested on a mat of woven rushes. Rudely shaped flint tools and relics of ancient clay pots were close by. In the late 1800s, such a discovery was awesome, especially since archaeologists believed the man lived in the Nile Valley some 7,000 years earlier. As the excavations continued, there were more finds of primitive bones and artifacts.

CRADLE OF CIVILIZATION

The fertile valley of the Nile was the cradle of our civilization. Historians and scholars may vary in their compilations of a factual chronology, nevertheless Egypt is the mother country of antiquity. Neolithic farming villages have shown the first signs of a long-lived culture concentrated along the river's middle and lower reaches. It was a way of life based on a finely balanced control of natural and human resources. Art, history, and letters were born here.

In the Late Predynastic period (circa 3100 B.C.) a vast river flowed from the northeast corner of Africa and carved the Nile Valley out of sandstone and limestone. Seasonal flooding cut the valley into ragged cliffs and terraces. Each year during the months of July through September, the river inundated the valley floor, leaving silt and mud to slowly create the upper Nile Delta. Reinforced by heavy flows and sunshine, the soil was fertile. Village communities clustered along its banks. Farmers tilled fields of green and cultivated food crops. The Nile was their lifeline.

Songs of praise linked the Nile to the ancient Egyptians' gods and their very existence. When there were seasons of little flooding and the desert sun scorched their land, weary farmers appealed to their gods in prayer and verse, such as in "The Ancient Hymn to the Nile, as told by Bernadette Menu in *Ramessess II: Greatest of the Pharaoh*:

> Lord of the fish, he sends wildfowl flying south, and no birds falls prey to the storm wide; He fathers the barley, brings emmer to be, fills the god's temples with odor of festival. But let him be backward, then breathing falters, all faces grow fierce with privation, Should the god's primal shrines lie dry in the dust, men by the millions were lost to mankind.

The discovery of human relics indicated that these were small people with dark hair who believed in some form of afterlife. This conclusion was reached because of numerous artifacts found buried alongside human skeletons—crudely made hand axes, bits of clothing, broken pottery, and food—intended not for this life, but the hereafter. These were the ancestors of Ramses II, greatest of all Egyptian pharaohs.

THE CHIEF DEITIES OF ANCIENT TIMES

In Late Predynastic period, the time of Re, Ka, and Narmer began. Re was the sun god, the king of the gods and father of humankind, and the chief deity of ancient Egypt. He was represented by the lion, cat, and falcon; wore the solar disk; and held an ankh and scepter. Ka was referred to as the soul of Egyptian mythology. Narmer was the falcon king of Upper Egypt who merged Upper and Lower Egypt into one realm. The falcon god Horus embodied one of the most fundamental tenets of Egyptian religious and political beliefs, and governed divine kingship. Ancient Egyptian rulers were followers of Horus, who by the time of unification of Upper and Lower Egypt, *was* the ruler of Egypt.

The falcon kings wore a tall miter known as the white crown. In the delta, the rival king wore the red crown, a flat-top cap with a front spiral with its back projected upward. After unification, the king, or pharaoh, wore a double crown. During battles he wore a blue crown.

Some Egyptologists believe Narmer to be king of the First Dynasty; others assimilate him as Narmer/Menes. (It is important to understand that historians vary in their assemblage of dates and variations in spelling. Contrary to the assumed north and south designations, Lower Egypt was called the north, while Memphis and Upper Egypt were considered to be in the southern portion.)

EARLY DYNASTIC PERIOD

Aha Menesof Tanis founded the First Dynasty (circa 2950–2575 B.C.) and its capital, the city of Memphis. Thus began the long line of pharaohs. The tombs of all the First Dynasty

Ancient Egyptians considered Re to be the father of all the gods. Often represented in lion, cat, or falcon form, it is said that Re created mankind from his own tears. Re *(above)* is depicted as a cat fighting his enemy snake god Apophis, the god of darkness.

kings were discovered at Abydos in Upper Egypt. The Thinite kings of Upper Egypt were buried close by. Historian Robert Guisepi commented on the relationship between a monarch and his afterlife: "the whole life of the Egyptian was spent in contemplation of death; thus the tomb became their concrete thought." Because of such a strong belief, their tombs were furnished with food and clothing, exotic jewelry, precious gems, fine furniture, pets, and sometimes their servants."

Egyptians believed their kings were divine, acting as middlemen between the people and the gods, and also that they were living images of Re, the sun god. The sovereigns spent hours contemplating religious rituals and associating themselves by name and symbolism with various gods. At his coronation, a king reenacted the events of creation. He swore to conquer Seth, god of chaos, and establish Maat, order, justice, and truth personified by Re's daughter. For example, Sethos I (Ramses' father), was connected to the name of the god known as Seth. Conducting many of the sacred ceremonies were the high priests. They were closest to the pharaohs, held religious power, performed rituals, read papyrus scrolls to the people, cared for the statues of gods, and composed magical texts to help a person into the afterlife.

Osiris, King of the Dead

Egyptians believed the god Osiris, king of the dead, dwelled at Abydos. Even if they had a tomb elsewhere, thousands of people sought to be buried there. They would arrange to have their mummy brought to Abydos and believed that to be buried near Osiris even for a short sojourn secured a greater afterlife.

Ancient myth held that Osiris was killed by his brother Seth. Isis, queen of the gods and sister and wife of Osiris, called in Anubis, god of the dead and the embalmer, to prepare the body for burial. Her charms, recited over Osiris, were so powerful that life returned and he went down to the underworld alive and became its king.

Within the Early Dynastic period there were the First, Second, and Third dynasties with a total of 17 kings. It was an era of mythology and magnificent accomplishments. If Aha, Narmer, and Menes were the same, Nicolas Grimal pointed out in *A History of Ancient Egypt*, "he was the inaugurator of the cult of the crocodile-god Sobek in the Faiyum region as well as the founder of Memphis . . . and probably had established both his administration and the cult of the Apsi-bull at Memphis." The Two

Ladies, Nekhbet, the vulture goddess of the south, and Wadjet, the cobra goddess of the north, were Menes' protectorates.

Menes, First King of Egypt

The kingdom of Menes rose significantly and rapidly. During his reign, he introduced the most progressive form of civilization thus far, enhancing religion, customs, art expression, architecture, and social culture. Although the country was occupied by various monarchies thereafter, over a period of nearly 3,000 years, Egypt itself remained remarkably stable and changed little. It ended with the Roman era of Augustus Caesar.

Menes' reign is remembered for several notable events: land surrounding the lower Nile was reclaimed after an immense dike was built. His royal army engaged in brutal raids against the Nubians in the south around Aswan, enabling Menes to expand his sphere of influence 600 miles (965.6 km). Here, the Nile tumbled over granite boulders of the first cataract (waterfalls).

Menes was married to Queen Berenib. He had one son and heir, Djer, mothered by a woman named Beithotepe. At age 63, Menes died. His death remains a mystery. Legend holds he was attacked by wild dogs and huge Nile crocodiles in Faiyum, a lush paradise on the edge of the Arabian Desert. After his suspicious death and burial at Saqqara, Djer became king.

THE PYRAMID AGE

The Old Kingdom (circa 2575–2150 B.C.), began in the Fourth Dynasty, and ended with the Eighth Dynasty. During this long era, there were 26 pharaohs who ruled with immense power and reaped tremendous wealth. They owned all the land, decided when farmers should plant their crops, took any surplus, and taxed the harvest.

"All things fear time," wrote famed world traveler Burton Holmes, "but time fears the pyramids." The earliest pyramids, and the oldest works of man, marked the frontiers between the unknown and the known. During the Third through Sixth

Dynasties, known as the Pyramid Age, Egyptians believed their god king must be preserved for his afterlife. This led to the ritual of mummification of the human body before its burial in a magnificent tomb.

King Djoser and his minister Imhotep designed and built the first monumental stone buildings in the world. The Step Pyramid was located in Saqqara, 10 miles (16 km) south of Cairo. It had a vast enclosure of satellite buildings, a tomb, and a palace. Imhotep's own tomb was there, and it was the nucleus of the Aesklepieion, an ancient center of healing . Pyramid construction provided work for farmers when the Nile flooded and for thousands of slaves captured during a pharaoh's recurring campaigns.

In the Fourth Dynasty, King Snofu built himself two geometric and beautiful pyramids with smooth sides. "Henceforth, the pharaoh's soul ascended a ramp like the sun's rays, not a stairway, to heaven," wrote Kenneth A. Kitchen in *Pharaoh Triumphant: The Life and Times of Ramses II.*

Snofu's son Cheops, also known by the name Khufu, built the Great Pyramid at Giza, the largest of all the tombs and the one survivor of the Seven Wonders of the World. It is a perfectly proportioned mountain of stone, as high as a 40-story building, with more than two million blocks of granite, each averaged about two and a half tons. The three pyramids at Giza were surrounded by streets of lesser tombs called mastabas, oblong rooms with sloping sides that connected with mummy chambers underground. These belonged to officers and dignitaries who would attend their masters' courts in the hereafter.

During the fifth century B.C., Greek historian Herodotus visited the tombs and was told by priests, "that when Cheops succeeded to the throne he plunged into all manner of wickedness. . . . He closed the temples and forbade the Egyptians to offer sacrifice, compelling them instead to labor, one and all, in his service. He commandeered the people of the Nile Valley to build the pyramid for him and ground them down to the lowest point of misery. . . . One hundred thousand men labored

Scribes' Training and Future

Scribes were credited with recording not only numerous personal stories, but the royal court's documents. Hieroglyphics, their system of writing, revealed vivid and accurate accounts of military battles, the number of killed or captured, activities of the royal court, the collection of taxes, and government records—a magnificent storage of dated events that occurred over three centuries.

This Egyptian treasury was the work of dedicated scribes, boys and men trained to accurately inscribe history on the stone walls of tombs, temples, monuments, and scrolls of papyrus. Most of the boys came from artisan or merchant families. Becoming a scribe could raise them above their parents' social class. Very few came from peasant families. As scribes, they were high on the Egyptian social scale.

Scribe schools were run by priests, and boys started at the early age of five. Typically they spent 12 years learning the symbols used in the complicated writing system. Students memorized 700 hieroglyphs and practiced copying them over and over until they were proficient. They practiced on pieces of wool, flakes of alabaster, and broken bits of pottery. When their technique was approved, they were allowed to write on papyrus. They carried a tablet in a leather bag slung over their shoulders. The bag contained tools. Finely sharpened reeds were used for pens, with two ink wells, one black and the other red. A small container held water used to wet the ink. They carried rolls of papyrus to be used as paper. To make papyrus, the inner part of the reed was stripped and soaked in water until soft. It was then laid out on the table in a crisscross pattern between two sheets of cloth. The strips were pressed together until the cloth had absorbed all the water. The strips were then pressed once more to form a sheet of paper. Sheets were flattened on a wood or stone table.

Studying to be a scribe was not an easy life. Classes lasted from dawn to sunset. Teachers were strict. A beating for mistakes was not unusual. Women were not allowed to become scribes, but some were taught to read and write.

constantly, and were relieved every three months by a fresh lot. It took ten years' of oppression for the people to make the causeway for the conveyance of the stones. The pyramid itself was twenty years in building," said Robert Guisepi, quoting the ancient Greek historian.

Cheops's successor was just as wicked, acknowledges Elizabeth Payne in *The Pharaohs of Ancient Egypt*. According to Payne, Herodotus wrote, "The Egyptians so detest the memory of these kings that they do not much like even to mention their names." Belief in the mortality of their kings remains controversial. Other historians reason that the men's arduous work was not slave labor. Rather, because they believed in the morality of their divine kings, building their tombs showed an act of faith.

Perhaps the most famous Egyptian monument aside from the pyramids is the Sphinx. Built in stone, it has an image of a recumbent lion with a stony semblance of a human face. It was considered the official guardian of Giza's Second Pyramid. Egyptian builders made expeditions to the Syrian coast to gather the prized cedar of Lebanon for its temple doors and to the Sinai to mine copper, gold, and turquoise to enhance the tomb's splendor.

Internal and external conflict erupted. Asiatic people penetrated the delta. Insurgent raids and foreign infiltration increased, and the mammoth construction projects were interrupted. The pharaoh's rule waned. Nile floods failed. In the First Intermediate period (circa 2125–1975 B.C.), the country split and civil war turned the land and its people into enemies. "Each man's heart is for himself," Robert Guisepi wrote. "A man sits with his back turned, while one slays another."

THE MIDDLE KINGDOM

In the Middle Kingdom (about 2000 to 1800 B.C.), there was a period of reunification. Egyptians made outstanding achievements in literature, art, architecture, and public works. In

The Step Pyramid of King Djoser *(above)* was the first structure of its kind, and provided the model for future royal tombs. Designed by the Djoser's minister Imohtep, this pyramid, as well as the ones built after it, is supposed to resemble the royal palace.

the marshy Faiyum area, engineers reclaimed 27,000 acres of arable land for farming. As a show of democracy, the pharaohs granted ordinary citizens immortality, the right to be mummified, and an afterlife.

In the late 1800s, robbers digging near the edge of the Egyptian desert unearthed a mummified crocodile, then a second, and a third. What they had stumbled upon was a crocodile cemetery. In ancient times, these animals were worshiped and sacrificed to Sobek, the crocodile god. They were buried in special cemeteries around small temples. "I am the Crocodile god, who dwelleth amid (the dead man's) terror. I am the Crocodile god, and I seize my prey like a ravening beast," National Geographic's *Treasures of Egypt* quoted from the Egyptian Book of the Dead.

THE NEW KINGDOM

Often called the Golden Age (circa 1539–1075 B.C.), Egypt again enjoyed a time of peace and stability during the New Kingdom. Foreign trade increased, and gigantic monuments were built. In 1279 B.C. the long reign of Ramses II, Son of Light, began.

Prince Ramses had been challenged many times by his father. Each time he proved deserving of his birthright. At 14 he had his first taste of war. Pharaoh Sethos had received news of unrest in Libya. This was too close to home, believed Sethos, who geared up a campaign to squelch the confrontation. Ramses joined his father in the ensuing battle. Kenneth A. Kitchen wrote, "he was probably not allowed too close to the firing line, but it was a beginning."

Determined to subdue other insurgents and to regain Egypt's former dominions, Qadesh and Amurru in Syria, Sethos planned yet another summer campaign, this time against the Hittites. With his father's formidable Egyptian army of charioteers, Ramses sailed to Phoenicia, where they stormed the east Anatolian land. Although they captured the two cities, the battle turned into a stalemate. King Muwatallis, the aggressive Hittite sovereign, and Pharaoh Sethos I mutually settled the conflict. Sethos gained back a portion of his domain but agreed to no further attempts to regain Qadesh and Amurru.

RAMSES THE ROYAL SCRIBE

Back in Memphis, Prince Ramses completed his education. He became a royal scribe with all its benefits: an apartment, servants, food, special privileges, and more than adequate enumeration. Handsome, slim, tanned by the sun, and battle seasoned, he had the strength of a young lion. Already he gave the impression of royal power, which enhanced his popularity among the elite, the wealthy, and pretty Egyptian girls.

Green-eyed Isetnofret proclaimed her love for Ramses. According to legend, she was the most beautiful girl he had ever seen. The couple shared idyllic moments and appeared together at country festivals and royal celebrations. But again, legend holds that the prince told friends he did not love her. According to poems Ramses later had inscribed on the tomb wall of Abu Simbel, it was the sensitive fifteen-year-old harem dancer and weaver Nefertari who captured his heart.

3

Ramses Crowned King of Egypt

CARVED ON A FADED SIENNA MURAL IN THE EXQUISITE TEMPLE OF ABYDOS is a chronological list that shows the names of every dynastic pharaoh from King Menes to Sethos I. King Sethos built the temple in honor of his royal ancestors, and each king's name was written in an oval-shaped lozenge or cartouche on the *Table of Abydos*. To the left of the names are the figures of Pharaoh Sethos and his young son, Ramses II. They appear to study the names and offer praise to the past kings. To ensure protection of his fine temple, Sethos issued a curse that was engraved on the tomb wall. "As for any official, who shall encourage his lord to remove the personnel for other service . . . he shall be doomed to the fire—it shall burn up his body, it shall devour his limbs! . . . any one who shall be deaf to this decree, Osiris shall pursue him, Isis will be after his wife, and Horus chase his children—all great ones of the Necropolis shall execute judgment against him!" It was a stern warning to future grave robbers, as recorded in Kitchen's *Pharaoh Triumphant: The Life and Times of Ramses II.*

PRINCE REGENT

Sethos I must have believed his son and heir to the throne, now in his late teens, should have more responsibility. Therefore, before a full royal court, Sethos bestowed Ramses the title of prince regent with all the royal trappings of a king and a crown. In *Pharaoh Triumphant: The Life and Times of Ramses II,* Kitchen said that years later, inscribed on Ramses' necropolis, appeared his words:

> When my father appeared to the populace, I being just a youth in his embrace, he spoke concerning me: Cause him to appear as King, that I may see his beauty while I yet live! . . . 'he shall direct this land, he shall attend to (its affairs), he shall command the populace' . . . because so great was the love for me within him.
>
> He furnished me with a household from the Royal Harim, comparable with the 'beauties' of the Palace; he selected for me wives . . . and concubines brought up in the Harim.

As befitting his son, Sethos gave Ramses the title Usi-am-re, meaning "Strong in Right is Re," and "Rameses II beloved of Amun." With his new authority, several important figures became part of the prince regent's life. Amen-em-inet became his personal retainer and companion, and Asha-hebsed became a commandant of troops. Both were friends from school.

BUILDER AND WARRIOR

While Sethos was putting down minor rebellions against the Nubian rebels or searching for gold to support his army,

Ramses had other work. He undertook the management of a black marble quarry at Aswan, oversaw sculpting of a magnificent gold statue of Sethos for the Osiris temple, and made preliminary designs for other splendid monuments, such as his own temple to Osiris. There were projects at Thebes; frequent inspections of goldsmiths, silversmiths, and stone carvers creating statues of the pharaoh, his children, animals, and sphinxes; artists delicately painting vases and urns; and woodcrafters who created exquisite ebony armchairs inlaid with gold and silver. These were all splendid furnishings for the king's monuments.

Architects, skilled in mathematics, worked out complex patterns. Captive slaves and workers dragged huge stones to the sites to begin foundations. Due to the many years it took to build these prominent effigies, Ramses had a village built to house workers and their families. Some remained their entire lives.

MARRIAGE, FAMILY, AND WARFARE

In the palace, Ramses married his first royal wife, Nefertari, who presented his firstborn son. His secondary wife, Isetnofret, gave birth to a second boy. There were more sons and daughters, and a nursery blossomed in the harem. King Sethos became grandfather to a dozen or so children. In ancient times, many babies died in infancy. Those who survived later played major and minor roles in Egyptian history. All of Ramses' boys held the title of commander and chief of the army. Ramses' brother and Sethos's heir apparent had died.

During the thirteenth year of Sethos's reign, Ramses, who was about 20 years old, participated in a military campaign to quell a minor revolt in lower Nubia (now Sudan). Already showing signs that he intended his sons to be brave and fearless warriors like himself, two of his two young sons, in the care of a charioteer, accompanied him. Boldly, he charged his chariot into the heart of battle. His two children, four-year-old crown

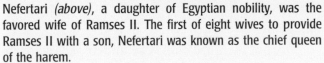

Nefertari *(above)*, a daughter of Egyptian nobility, was the favored wife of Ramses II. The first of eight wives to provide Ramses II with a son, Nefertari was known as the chief queen of the harem.

prince Amunherwenemef, and Ramses' fourth son, three-year-old Khaemwaset, followed, standing proudly in their chariots. Here was their first introduction to violence and the thrill of the "charge." Afterward, Ramses ordered a small rock temple built at Beit el-Wali to commemorate his family's triumph. The conquest was dramatized on its stone walls and was portrayed as a magnificent victory. It showed Ramses accepting the spoils of war: bags of gold dust, animal pelts, weapons, and domestic and wild animals. Another scene showed him standing in his exquisite horse-drawn chariot, arms outstretched with bow and arrow, quiver at his waist, pet lion at his side, and thousands of Nubians felled in his wake.

In his second year as crown regent, Ramses dealt with myriad attacks by Sherden pirates, a mixed group of renegade seafarers from the Mediterranean islands. Accompanied by their families, who probably intended to settle in Egypt, they raided the delta, destroyed villages, and killed hundreds of innocent farmers. Firm in his commitment to defend all Egypt and uphold his royal title, Prince Ramses was determined to halt their unscrupulous marauding. He sent armed troops to the delta and anchored ships fueled with combat-trained sailors near the mouth of the Nile. Not expecting any land or sea defense, the enemy assaulted the delta. Surprised by the massive Egyptian defense, they were ill prepared for an all-out battle. Overwhelmed on both sea and land, they were killed or were captured and conscripted into the Egyptian military. Their families became slaves.

MAGIC OF OSIRIS

In the sixteenth year of his reign, King Sethos suddenly died. Prince Ramses became the uncontested monarch of all Egypt. He was 22, the year 1279 B.C. Ramses was born during the reign of Horemheb, before his grandfather ascended the throne. At the time, Ramses I and Sethos were simply high government officials. Although Sethos was obviously king when Ramses II was crowned coregent, his election resembled that of Horemheb. Clearly the succession of the crown prince was not a foregone or inherited conclusion and had to be secured while his father was alive. Only later, when Ramses II ruled alone, did he revert to the old "myth of the birth of the divine king" that had legitimized rulers of the Eighteenth Dynasty.

According to ancient Egyptian beliefs, mummification was necessary to ensure a dead person's entrance to the afterlife. Before Ramses' coronation, there were 70 days to prepare King Sethos's mummy for burial. While plans for the funeral were being made, to show respect for their beloved pharaoh, the ordinary man in the streets let his beard grow, and women

Mummification

Ancient Egyptians believed that mummification guaranteed a safe passage to the afterlife. The more elaborate preparations were for royalty, their families, high priests, and others of wealthy stature. The process was performed by embalmers and took 70 days. The body was first cleansed and purified, and then the inner organs—the liver, intestines, lungs, and stomach—were removed. To prevent decay, the organs were placed in natron, a compound of sodium carbonate and sodium bicarbonate used to dry out the corpse. The organs were then wrapped in linen strips and placed in four canopic jars. The body cavity was stuffed with additional natron. The embalmers believed the heart was the center of a person and the central point of intelligence. It was placed on a scale. Forty-two gods weighed the heart against a feather. If the scales balanced, the deceased could enter the underworld and enjoy a peaceful afterlife in the kingdom of Osiris; if the scales tilted, the goddess, Devourer of the Dead, would eat the heart and the deceased would die a second, permanent death.

The brain and surrounding tissue were next. The embalmer inserted a hooked instrument through the nostrils and pulled out bits of brain tissue, a delicate procedure performed with extreme care so as not to disfigure the face. The brain was considered unimportant. The body wore their hair down. Important court decisions were put on hold. Ramses, however, announced the royal summer palace at Avaris would become the new city of Piramses and the capital of Egypt.

Finally, in late summer, a brilliant flotilla of royal ships set sail for the Valley of the Kings. "The great fleet turned north, rowed downstream by ranks of practiced mariners whose oars sung in unison like the legs of great gold water-beetles upon the

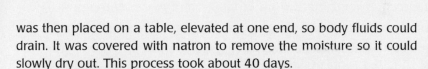

was then placed on a table, elevated at one end, so body fluids could drain. It was covered with natron to remove the moisture so it could slowly dry out. This process took about 40 days.

After the body was sufficiently dried and appeared sunken, the natron was removed and the body was washed. To make the body more lifelike, pieces of linen were inserted in sunken parts and false eyes were placed in the eye cavities. The body was then wrapped in hundreds of yards of linen. Each appendage was wrapped individually. Often a mask of the deceased's likeness was placed on the face and wrapped separately. Throughout the process of wrapping, the mummy was coated with resin. Good-luck amulets and prayers of wisdom were tucked between the layers. When finished, the mummy was wrapped in a shroud.

To complete the procedure, a priest used a special instrument to touch parts of the body to open its senses for the afterlife. This was called Opening of the Mouth. This allowed the ba and the ka (the soul and the vital essence) to travel to the next world. Finally the body was sealed in a coffin or sarcophagus (a stone coffin) and placed in the burial chamber. The interior of the coffin might have been brightly decorated with images of underworld gods. The outside was ablaze with colorful hieroglyphics to help the person in the kingdom of Osiris.

green and bluish waters," wrote Christian Jacq in *The Eternal Temple*. The great royal wife Tuya led the cortege with Nefertari and Ramses at her side.

When the ships arrived at Abydos, Ramses, clad in a panther's skin and golden sandals, led the way to his father's tomb. Twelve high priests carried the gold coffin, followed by a procession of servants with offerings of splendid furnishings. Sethos's reign ended when the hand-hued tomb doors were sealed. The long and illustrious reign of Ramses II was about to begin.

RAMSES' SPIRITUAL BAPTISM

Six years before his death, Sethos had taken his son to Abydos to the great tomb of Osiris at Thebes to be initiated into the mysteries of the King of the Dead. Ramses and his father respectfully entered the tomb complex and passed through two broad hypostyle halls to the inner courtyard. There the high priests of Osiris washed the young prince's hands and feet. They then led him through massive cedar of Lebanon gilded doors, to the seven sanctuaries. A statue of Maat stood before each chapel as a dedication to the pharaoh and the gods. Woven reed baskets filled with fresh fruit and bouquets of white lilies and lotus blossoms lay at the statues' feet. Incense scented the cool air that wafted with the immortal essence of ka. In the Gallery of Lists they passed the beautifully engraved cartouches of the previous 67 pharaohs. A frieze of muted gold, deep blue green, and red showed young Ramses roping the wild bull. Behind the temple, and unseen by and forbidden to many, was the tomb of Osiris.

They entered by underground rock steps, past an arched passageway, to a vaulted hall supported by massive monolithic pillars. In the center was a raised mound surrounded by a channel of subterranean water. Sethos explained that the mound represented the emergence of Osiris from the energy of the ocean. The water symbolized the Nile, rain, and the desert

When Osiris *(above center)* was killed, he was sent to rule over the underworld with his fellow god, Anubis *(above left)*. Together they watched over the dead, while Osiris's son, Horus, became the patron god of the living pharaohs. This detail from the ancient Egyptian Stele of Nanai shows the deceased adoring Osiris and Anubis.

artesian wells. He instructed Ramses to "immerse himself in the ocean so that his spirit would step beyond the visible world, and he would draw strength from that which has neither beginning nor end," wrote Christian Jacq in *The Son of Light*.

In this mythical occult ritual, Ramses drank from the invisible ocean and ate unseen wheat that grew from the mound. A jackal-masked priest, representing Anubis, protector of the dead, then directed the young prince to battle. In the guise of Horus, god of the sky and referred to as the Son of Light, Ramses had to beat back the devil Anubis. At last, exhausted from the spiritual ceremony, he collapsed. As a result of the nocturnal baptism of Osiris, the priest had united the prince with his divine essence and filled him with spiritual strength and resolve toward his responsibilities as king.

Osiris clearly played a double role: he was both a god of fertility and the embodiment of the dead and resurrected king. He granted all life, from the underworld to sprouting vegetation from the annual Nile floods. Around 2000 B.C., it was believed that every man at death, not just deceased kings, became associated with Osiris. The living king was identified as Horus. Thus Osiris and Horus were father and son.

THE CORONATION OF RAMSES II

On the eve of his coronation, Ramses and Nefertari prayed at the temple of Karnak. There he promised to uphold the laws of Maat, the goddess of truth, balance, and order. He was strengthened by thoughts of his father's great wisdom and benevolence and the sacred words of the gods.

Early the next morning, Ramses was bathed and cleansed with unguents and dressed in a kilt of white and gold. The priests hung a bull's tail on his sash, the emblem of royal potency and the bull's power. Next they fashioned a jeweled collar with six strands of beads to his neck, copper bracelets were placed on his wrists and upper arms, and white sandals were put on his feet. He was given a white club to strike down his enemies. Last, they tied a golden band called a *sia* around his forehead for intuitive seeing. His coronation began.

The priests lifted two crowns to his head, the red crown and the white crown of Upper and Lower Egypt. Ramses was directed to sit upon the royal throne, sculptured of mahogany and overlaid with gold leaf. The queen mother, portrayed as the goddess Isis, bowed low to him and said, "May Your Majesty rise like a new sun and take his place on the throne of the living." Then, as told by Christian Jacq in *The Son of Light*, she chanted his five royal titles:

Strong Bull, Beloved of Maat,
Protector of Egypt, He Who Binds up Foreign lands,
Rich in Armies, Powerful in Victories,
Chosen of the God of Light, Powerful in His Rule,
Ra-Begot-Him: Son of Light."

Afterward the queen mother beckoned Nefertari to take her place beside Ramses as queen of Egypt. As befitting the conclusion of the coronation, King Ramses set a crown with two feathered plumes on Nefertari and declared her his great royal wife.

4

Daily Life in Ancient Egypt

THE MIGHTY NILE IS THE LONGEST RIVER IN THE WORLD AT 4,187 MILES (6,738.3 km) long, 1,000 miles (1,609.3 km) longer than Brazil's Amazon River. For more than 5,000 years, the river has provided livelihood to settlers in the Nile Valley and the delta. Perhaps the ancient Greek historian Herodotus best described it when he called it "Gift of the Nile."

Egypt is situated in the northeastern corner of the African continent. It is largely desert and gets little rainfall. It is the twelfth largest country in Africa and about the size of Texas and California. Sudan borders Egypt in the south; Libya is to the west; the Mediterranean Sea is to the north; and Israel, the Gulf of Aqaba, and the Red Sea are to the east.

Hapi was god of fertility and the Nile. In predynastic times, the river was called Hapi and people believed he worked for the pharaohs. But, in the years when the river did not overflow its banks, Hapi was depicted as a destructive power. Ancient lore recounts that the Nile flowed through the land of the dead and the heavens and finally coursed into Egypt and rose out of the ground between two mountains of the islands of Abu (Elephantine) and Iat-Rek (Phile).

As the yearly flood time approached, the entire valley grew increasingly anxious. They carried statues of Hapi around the villages for all to honor. When the river overflowed its banks and flooded the ancient land, they threw amulets into the water and prayed that its inundation would not be too high or too low. If there was not enough water for their fields or livestock, they believed the gods were angry and refused to send water. Wind scoured the land, their crops died, and famine crippled the land.

Millions of people have used the Nile for farming, drinking, trading, and transporting travelers and industrial and commercial goods to foreign lands. Downstream currents proved easy sailing. To navigate upstream, sails were hoisted to prevailing winds and oarsmen kept a steady beat. A thousand years before Ramses II, Pepi I built the first major shipping canal. Warriors, armed with bows and arrows, set sail to conquer neighboring lands. To keep their hold on Nubia and open the Nile farther, the Egyptian infantry pierced the rocks of the first cataract at Aswan.

The river provided another kind of transportation. Gigantic stones were ferried from nearby quarries for the construction of pyramids and temples. Later the canals were widened so sizeable ships could haul huge blocks of granite and obelisks downriver.

A NILOMETER TO MEASURE WATER DEPTH

So important was the lifeblood of the Nile to Egyptians that early on they began to keep records of the river's crest. Since

In ancient Egypt, the nilometer was developed to measure the depths of the Nile River. Using this system, officials were able to predict each region's harvest and taxed each area according to their crop. Three nilometers are still located in Egypt, including one at Elephantine Island *(above)*, but are useless due to dams on the Nile River.

recorded time, the island of Rawdah at Cairo has been a large port, an arsenal, a fortress, the site of royal palaces, and the Nilometer. This unusual octagonal column was divided into cubits (the royal cubit, almost 52 centimeters, was the base of the official Egyptian measuring system). The Nilometer was located in the middle of a square stone-lined shaft. It measured the extent of the Nile flood to calculate farmers' crop success or failure. A rise of less than six meters (one cubit) might cause dearth and hardship; eight meters predicted a plentiful harvest. The Nilometer thus provided the pharaohs a way to calculate the amount of taxes to impose. Temples built along the Nile had staircases that led down to the river to measure the water level.

The source of the Nile is the Kagera River in Burundi. The Nile travels through nine African nations before reaching the Mediterranean Sea. It flows through four lakes—Victoria, Kyoga, Albert, and Nasser. Along the way it is fed by important tributaries such as the Blue Nile, the White Nile, and the Atbara. At Cairo, the river widens into fields and sandbars of the delta, a large triangle region at the mouth of the Nile. After unification of Upper and Lower Egypt, King Menes had dug more elaborate formations of basins to contain the flood waters, and canals, ditches, dikes, and levees. Hundreds of waterways split into channels with two main tributaries, the Rosette and Damietta. Sixty percent of Egyptian land is in the delta. Fertile land was called Black Land, which referred to its rich, dark silt.

THE VAST SAHARA DESERT

South of Cairo the Nile Valley is cut into cliffs of granite, sandstone, and limestone. Between the Nile River and the Red Sea is the wind-scoured Arabian Eastern Desert, once a fertile area. Fossilized trees litter the remains of a million years ago. Valleys called wadi were once riverbeds. Desert areas were called the Red Land.

Two-thirds of Egypt is part of the Western Desert, the great Sahara. It stretches across northern Africa from the Atlantic coast to the Nile Valley. Shifting sand dunes appear to move with unpredictable desert winds. In scattered patches of green are oases. For thousands of years, people have used these sheltered places to grow date palms and water their livestock. Daytime temperatures can rise as high as 120 degrees Fahrenheit (48.8 degrees Celsius), nights can be below freezing, and venomous snakes, scorpions, and lizards infest the ever-changing terrain. Judging by the structure of the land and its unpredictable Nile, it became clear why ancient people relied on Hapi to survive.

The Sinai Peninsula was once a formidable barrier between Egypt and the Middle East. It was bordered by the Mediterranean in the north, the Gulf of Aqaba in the east, and the Suez in the west. It was here that Ramses II, like his father, Sethos I, mined precious turquoise and copper, and used the barren landscape for cargo routes and troop movements to foreign lands.

ANCIENT PEOPLE

Ancient Egyptians are believed to have belonged to the eastern branch of a people known as the Hamites. They were said to be descendants of Ham, the youngest of the biblical Noah's three sons, the original speakers of the Hamitic language. The Fellahin (farmers in Arab countries) have been described as the true Egyptians and the oldest people of civilization. They lived in small villages along the riverbanks. Their houses were made of bundles of reeds coated with chopped straw and silt from the ditches. Palm fronds covered the roofs and provided protection from the extreme elements. With crudely made hoes, hand axes, and sickles, they farmed the rich topsoil and raised barley, corn, onions, a coarse grain called cyllestis, and flax for meal and fabric. They kept goats, sheep, and water buffaloes; made bread in clay ovens or open fires; and ate dried fish and wild fowl. Mulberries, gathered from the marshes, were used for lamp oil. When men ventured into the Nile to fish, they sailed in lightweight river skiffs made from papyrus. Ancient tomb art depicts a single man, standing at the bow, holding a long pole to fend off the river's inevitable crocodile or rhinoceros.

"Food, bread, beer, and all good things," is a phrase found engraved on a funerary stele and used by the host to inform his guests. The stele provided historians with an ancient menu. Greek historian Herodotus took it a step further and wrote,

"They eat loaves of bread of coarse grain which they call cyl-lestis. They made their beverage from barley, for they had no vines in their country, ate fish raw, sun-dried or preserved in salt brine." Foods were served in pottery bowls painted with ducks and deer and on exquisite alabaster dishes.

The bedouins were the wanderers, sometimes called nomads, who traditionally dwelled in the Western and Sinai deserts. They lived in tribes and moved herds of camels and flocks of sheep from oasis to oasis to find suitable pastures. They ate lamb and rice, and their camels supplied a source of milk. From camel hair they made tents, carpets, and their clothes. The head of the tribe was called a sheik. Although bedouins led a primitive and largely isolated life, the women could engage in business and choose their husbands. In ancient times, they were often predaceous and known to plunder from raids on other settlements, passing caravans, and one another.

Nubian people came from northern Sudan and lived along the Nile Valley near Aswan. Like the Fellahin, they made their homes from river mud and straw reeds. Their livelihood came from the dense thickets of date palms that grew along the river's edge. The palms furnished them with food and materials for timber and making rope. Nubians were also invaders who attempted to control Egypt. In turn, there were long periods during which Egyptian pharaohs, such as Ramses II, controlled and collected taxes from the Nubians. In armed conflict, the Nubians were highly skilled archers and fearless warriors who fought bitter battles against the imposing armies. Taken as prisoners, they were forced into slave labor in the brickfields or had to drag endless tons of stone for Ramses' great pylon gateway.

During the Middle Kingdom, Semitic-speaking people made their homes in Egypt. They worked as servants or members of Egyptian households, adapting to certain ways of their new masters. Pharaohs had strict control of immigrants and people who were already residents. Many came as prisoners of war: Canaanites, Amorites, and Hurrians. Others became slaves on the vast temple grounds. It they were fortunate, they might

Ancients Loved Their Flowers

Orchards and vineyards abounded with beauty, fragrance, and nourishment. Palace walls and ceilings were painted with offerings of flowers. Lovers offered their beloved flowers; victorious kings received nosegays. Flowers were the symbol of life, the beginning of creation. The lotus flower was the first blossom to emerge from the primordial waters. Harsomtus (another form of the god Horus) emerged in the form of a child or a snake from the lotus bloom. Uto was identified with the papyrus. Gods were thought to be in flowers and it was believed that their fragrance emanated from the divine. Wreaths contained branches of twigs chosen for fresh greenery and soothing fragrance.

Pliny the Elder (A.D. 23–79), Roman historian and scientist killed in the eruption of Vesuvius, described the excellent growing conditions in Egypt as suited for a horticulturalist. In *Naturalis Historia* he wrote, "In Egypt the leguminous plants appear as early as the third day after they are sown."

Farmers adapted early to the seasonal floods, the heat that followed, and climate conditions suitable for cultivating their crops. As trade with Asia and the Mediterranean islands expanded, foreign seeds and roots were introduced and a larger selection of vegetables and herbs broadened the Egyptian menu. Radish, sesame, lentils, chickpeas, lettuce, grapes, cucumbers, gourds, and herbs such as mustard, dill, cinnamon, rosemary, garlic, and cumin now flourished in fields and markets. New flavors and exotic dishes livened the palates of the wealthy. Egypt's three seasons provided an abundance of wild flowers: poppies, lupine, iris, daises, and heliotrope. Botanist Percy Newberry collected ancient seed in Egypt when he accompanied the famed archaeologist Flinders

work in government departments. The hungry or homeless immigrants came as compulsory slaves.

The Apiru were thought of as displaced, rootless people who easily mixed with others mentioned in the Bible. These

Petrie. In the nineteenth century seed from many horticultural expeditions were introduced in Europe.

Ramses' royal table might have included roast quail seasoned with dill and mustard, Nile perch with rosemary, honey cakes with sesame seeds, bread seasoned with cinnamon and raisins, and grape wine flavored with anise and coriander. Banquet guests dressed in fine linens. Men and women wore perfume and lined their eyes with green or black makeup. Women powdered their cheeks, wore ropes of beads, painted their nails, and used red lipstick. Musicians, dancers, and acrobats provided entertainment.

Those who had gardens adjacent to their homes grew a variety of vegetables and fruit such as pomegranates, figs, and dates. This type of cultivation was more difficult than the farmers' whose gardens lay along the Nile, for often the orchards and vineyards were on high ground, and water had to be drawn from the river and carried or carted to the garden and irrigated by hand.

> The gardener carries a yoke,
> His shoulders are bent as with age:
> There's a swelling on his neck
> And it festers,
> In the morning he waters vegetables,
> The evenings he spends with the herbs,
> While at noon he has toiled in the orchard.
> He works himself to death
> More than all other professions.
>
> —K.A. Kitchen, from M. Lichtheim's *Ancient Egyptian Literature*

people were probably Hebrews or clan groups from Israel. Their forefathers, Jacob and Joseph, had come to Egypt to escape the famine. According to Exodus 1:13–14, "So they made the people of Israel serve with rigor, and made their lives bitter with hard service, in mortar and brick, and all kinds of work in the field."

PYRAMIDS DICTATED TO SOCIAL POSITION

In Egypt's rigid social pyramid, pharaohs ruled the country and its subjects. Next were government officials, and then priests, who carried out the pharaoh's orders. Most came from noble families and enjoyed a high quality of life. Since religion was part of people's daily lives, the priests were in charge of the temples, sacred rituals, and ceremonies of death and burial.

Next were the scribes, who could read and write and held respected positions in society. Their job was to record information for the government, priests, high-ranking officials, and those willing to pay. After the scribes came the artisans, craftspeople, carpenters, metalworkers, painters, sculptors, and stone carvers.

At the bottom of the pyramid were the peasants and farm-workers who cultivated the land for the Egyptians. During the hot, dry climate of summer, when they did not farm, they worked on the pharaoh's colossal building projects.

THE BEAUTIFUL FEAST OF OPET

One of the first celebrations the newly crowned king of Egypt participated in was the Opet Festival, a lavish annual ceremony that lasted 27 days. It began near the beginning of the Nile's three-month flood season. To determine the date, a solar-corrected lunar calendar was consulted. For various purposes, ancient Egyptians used three calendars: the lunar, solar/sidereal, and civil. In prehistoric time, the lunar calendar had 12 months and 345 days. It was unsynchronized with the cycle of solar seasons, which is 365¼ days. The lunar calendar was adjusted by adding a thirteenth lunar month every three years or so. A solar-corrected lunar calendar was used to determine the festival dates.

The word "Opet" meant "secret chamber" and referred to the secluded rooms that adjoined the holy sanctuary of Amun-Re of Luxor in the innermost chamber of Amenotep III's temple. The room stood on a low mound considered to be the original Mound of Creation that rose out of the primeval waters. The festival celebrated the birth of the god Amun-Re. Recorded legend noted the gods had grown weary waiting for the agricultural cycle to complete its course. Fresh energy was needed. To accomplish this, priests drew from outside the created world to tap the pure and uncontrolled power of the boundless chaos surrounding the cosmos. Amum-Re was king of the gods and patron of pharaohs. Ramses identified with the god Re.

Prior to the celebration, priests decorated the sparkling golden barque of Amun of Karnak with flowers. They bathed and dressed the god in colorful linen and adorned the statue with bracelets, scepters, amulets of gold and silver, and other precious gems. The god was then enclosed in a shrine and placed on a ceremonial barque. It was then hoisted on to the shoulders of priests to begin the journey to Luxor. Accompanying the icon in their own barques were his wife, the goddess Mut, and their son, Knons. A flotilla of ships led by Ramses and his royal family in his golden royal barge set sail. The procession was followed by dignitaries, priests, solders, singers, acrobatic dancers, drummers, musicians, and chariots of the temple.

> Beautifully you shine forth, O Amen-Re, while you are in
>   the barge Userhat!
> All the people give you praise, the whole land is festivity.
> For your eldest Son and Heir sails you to Luxor.
> May you grant him Eternity as King of the Two lands,
> Everlasting in peaceful years.
> May you protect him with life, stability and dominion,
> May you grant him to appear in glory as the Joyful Ruler . . .
>
> —Kenneth A. Kitchen, *Pharaoh Triumphant*

After arriving at Luxor, the icons were moved into the temple. They were greeted by throngs of royals, priests, and

Amun-Re was the combination of two deities, the local god Amun and the king of the gods, Re. Most depictions of Amun-Re, such as the Eighteenth-Dynasty gilded silver statue *(above)*, show Amun crowned by double feathers and a solar disc, a symbol of Re.

peasants who offered flowers, food offerings, and fattened and decorated cattle destined to be sacrificed.

Ramses was purified with water, perfumed, and presented to Amun-Re. He repeated the sacred coronation rites. Priests then placed the two royal crowns, red and white, on his head. In the inner sanctuary, he made additional offerings to the god, to revitalize the god, and in response, the god revitalized the king. Afterward it was a time of gaiety and lavish nourishment.

A spectacular composite of the Opet processional was inscribed on the colonnade walls in Luxor. It showed priests generously distributing loaves of bread and jars of beer to the excited subjects. Handsomely carved on tall courtyard columns were mythical figures of small lapwing birds with human arms and hands raised in adoration seated on top of small baskets.

5

Master Builder

RAMSES SUCCEEDED HIS FATHER, SETHOS I, ON THE THRONE IN EITHER 1304 or 1279 B.C., depending on how the Sothic date in the Papyrus Ebers is interpreted. (Sothic pertained to Sirius, the Dog Star. The Papyrus Ebers was an early medical papyrus. Use of these documents enabled Egyptologists to set absolute dates for the entire period of pharaohs.)

No sooner had Ramses been crowned king of all Egypt than he began to draft significant and far-reaching plans for his reign. Unbeknown to the young pharaoh, mythical Egyptian gods had already sealed his legacy with grace and divine power called *sekhem*.

"His [Ramses'] reign was by far the most glorious and also the best known," wrote Nicolas Grimal. "Over a course of sixty-seven years he covered the Nile Valley with monuments and left an incredible mark on ancient Near Eastern history. His extraordinary personality was the primary influence on a period of memorable confrontations between the great Near Eastern empires."

Sethos had left the country in relative peace and prosperity, although there was some unsettled turmoil. He had restored the traditional temples and provided a splendid new setting for the annual Beautiful Feast of the Nile Valley. At Abydos, one of the oldest and holiest cities in all Egypt, he built a magnificent temple for the god Osiris with the distinguished Table of Abydos engraved on the hypostyle hall. Money for his massive building projects came from quarries and mines in the Sinai and Nubia, and copper-mining sites in Wadi Arabah and Wadi Mia in the Eastern Desert. He raided Nubia for captives to work as cheap or slave labor, and he was the first king to face the incursions of Libyan tribes along the western border of the delta. Later the tribes were believed to have been motivated by famine. Previous military confrontations with the Hittites had resulted in a negotiated peace agreement.

Under his father's tutelage, Ramses gained experience in the operation of Egypt's monarchy and the duties and responsibilities of a powerful sovereign. Now he was ready to implement his own role, both on the battlefield and to complete his father's temple in Karnak. It was traditional that after the coronation, the new pharaoh would begin his own tomb. This, too, was on Ramses' agenda.

Ramses' royal education; his keen interest in mathematics, chemistry, and science; and his dedication and daily prayers to the spiritual principals of Maat enhanced his overall expertise. With his father he participated in several campaigns against the Sherden pirates (also referred to as the Sea People) and quelled a rebellion in Nubia. The campaigns heightened his self-confidence and militaristic skills. His inherent belief in the god Amun-Re fulfilled his expected royal qualifications.

Still, at 22 years of age, Ramses was young, and minor skirmishes with other lands and their officials foreshadowed his future. People in his government questioned his leadership and judgment, as well as his ability to rule the vast kingdom of Egypt. Nevertheless, Ramses' youthful optimism and determination appeared to outweigh any criticism or resentment.

The first order of royal business was an ambitious building program. Next, he planned to conquer Egypt's vast empire. Nubia was still under Egyptian control, but the warlike Hittites had taken most of Syria back, and their intentions to invade Palestine were suspect.

Before all else, Ramses embarked on a grand ceremonial tour. Accompanied by his royal family and a fleet of gaily decorated ships, he commenced to greet the Egyptian people. Elated with the kingdom he had inherited, Ramses rode the rising Nile as if he were bringing the lifesaving waters to his people. At Thebes he paid his respect to his newly appointed high priest of Amun. He journeyed northward on the silver blue river to the next village and the next. Beyond the first cataract, he went to Abu Simbel, where later he would build one of the most famous temples in Egypt. Each time he was cheered and feasted by rich and poor. When he at last entered the delta, Ramses, tall and handsome in a linen kilt, double crown, and golden adornments, with his beautiful royal wife at his side, must have truly enchanted and radiated confidence for the welfare of the Egyptians.

Strategy and ambitious projects quickly consumed the new king's days. Besides his appointment of the high priest of Amun, he selected his vizier, Paser, who was a knowledgeable and trusted veteran of Sethos's reign. As vizier, he held power second only to the pharaoh. Neb-iot was Ramses' choice for chief treasurer. He was charged with the government's wealth and collecting taxes. Taxes were calculated according to a man's occupation and were received in grain, cows, cloth, silver, and even beer.

WORKERS' VILLAGE

Next, Ramses commanded all stonemasons, craftsmen, sculptors, and scribes to push forward with the great Hypostyle Hall of Columns at Karnak. He "stretched the cord" for the foundation of his own memorial temple, the Ramesseum, on the west bank of Thebes (now Luxor). His meticulously drawn plans called for huge statues and towering obelisks carved with the titles of kings and their dedication to their gods. The pointed tip of the obelisk represented the ground on which the sun god stood to create the universe. Two obelisks were designed for the entrance to the Luxor temple. Today, only one remains. In 1836, Pasha Mohammed Ali gave the other obelisk to the king of France. It is now in the Place de la Concorde, Paris. "The chiefs of all the foreign lands are beneath your sandals," declared the inscription, as recorded by Bernadette Menu in *Ramessess II: Greatest of the Pharaohs*. The statue of Ramses, with sandaled feet, symbolically showed him trampling the nine bows that represented the conquest of his foreign enemies.

Before his death, King Sethos had begun plans for a new temple at Aksha near the second cataract in Nubia. According to Kenneth A. Kitchen, "[H]ere was the cult of the king's and the living image of Ramsese II . . . the great god, Lord of Nubia." He was celebrated with the cult of Amun and Re. The cult was centered not on the worship of the king, but on his adoration and role as the godhead he represented.

To house and feed the hundreds of craftsmen and their families there were stone houses in a self-contained and isolated community known as the workers' village. The settlement was located halfway between the Valley of the Kings and Deir el-Medina. Villagers trudged a mile over the mountains to reach the monuments. Medina reached its final extant, with about 1,200 workmen, during Ramses' reign. Imagine the plot plan of an urban housing division with rows of houses neatly laid out off

Although Ramses II was educated by the best tutors and had experienced battles by his father's side, the priests still doubted his ability to rule Egypt. The young pharaoh had a number of plans in mind, including extensive construction goals that ultimately yielded glorious temples and stone reliefs dedicated to his reign *(above)*.

of streets and surrounded by a wall. Rather than two- or three-bedroom houses, however, these were smaller houses, more like two-room apartments. A worker's schedule included one day off every ten days. Because of the distance between the houses and monuments, settlements of small straw huts were built nearer the tombs where workers stayed while at work. Captive laborers lived in similar huts. Hillside chapels and burial grounds joined the community. The costs of food consumption and incidentals, such as water carriers who brought water to the village, were managed by the chief of the treasury.

Houses were assigned to workers in keeping with their positions and were intended for the educated and affluent. They were long and narrow, with whitewashed interiors and room to accommodate four people. Floors were uneven, perhaps due to the uneven mountainous terrain. A chair for the master stood on a raised platform. Beneath the platform was the entrance to a cellar for storing food and other perishables. The open-air cooking room contained an oven for baking bread, a kneading trough, and a mill or mortar. Sandals and household furnishings were made from reeds and rushes gathered from the river. There was no bathroom or fixed toilet. When a workman died, his widow lost the rights to the home.

These houses, or flats, were similar to the ones built at Giza during the Fourth Dynasty. Pharaoh Khufu ruled during the Old Kingdom. He is best known as the builder of the Great Pyramid. Khufu maintained full control of the workers' village and organized and fed as many as 20,000 workers. The pyramid took more than 20 years to complete.

Love poems found in an excavated workers' village on the outskirts of the Valley of Kings revealed emotional and sensitive phrases not much different than those of today's poets.

The Flower Song;
To hear your voice is pomegranate wine to me:
I draw life from hearing it.

Could I see you with every glance,
It would be better for me
Than to eat or to drink.

"People tend to assume all ancient Egyptian writing is religious, so the secular nature of these songs, and of much other poetry, continue to surprise readers," commented Richard Parkinson, an expert on ancient Egyptian poetry at London's British Museum. The poem was translated by M. V. Fox.

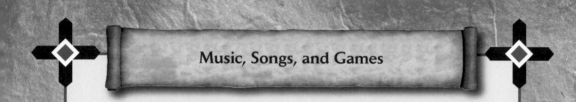

Music, Songs, and Games

Despite a profound belief in the hereafter and the sacred gods that controlled their lives and deaths, the Egyptians enjoyed their time on earth. Party scenes painted on tomb walls showed adults and children engaged in music, revelry, and sport. Much a part of their lives were festivals accompanied with spirited music, dancing, and feasting. Even the poorest, hardworking peasants made time to play.

An afternoon's entertainment might include youngsters singing bright notes or dancing to conflicting rhythms of bronze cymbals, bone clappers, tambourines, and castanets. Pretty girls strummed five-string harps. Musical lyrics extolled the beauties of nature or hymns to the gods. Robust dancers turned somersaults, and boys blew on reed flutes, perhaps accompanied by a lively cadence of brilliantly dressed processioners. Noblewomen and priestesses carried sacred rattles in praise of the goddess Hathor who liked music and dance.

Children played games similar to those of today, such as leapfrog and tug-of-war. Girls and boys threw balls, catching and tossing them to each other. Storytellers amused children and adults with frightening tales of hungry crocodiles, charging rhinoceroses, or slithering snakes. There were stories of the Wonders of the Magicians,

HUMAN SACRIFICES

Tomb hieroglyphics showed some extraordinary and varied characteristics of the ancient kings. Fourteen hundred years before Ramses built his tomb, King Aha chose a site at Abydos. According to National Geographic's *Treasures of Egypt*, legend tells that Aha was killed by a raging hippopotamus. On the day of his burial, six open graves were dug around his tomb. In a final act of devotion, or coercion, six people were poisoned and buried along with wine and food for the afterlife. One was

related to pyramid builders; General Sisenet, a detective yarn that took place during the reign of Pepi II; and Capture of Joppa, perhaps reminiscent of the story of Ali Baba and the Forty Thieves. Egyptian authors Hardjedef and Imhotep wrote fantasy, romantic, or adventure stories—*Tale of Two Brothers*, *Ghost Story*, and *The Foredoomed Prince*—on papyrus manuscripts. Animal tales, forever popular, suggested the source of Aesop's tale of the lion and rat called the *Myth of the Eye and the Sun*.

Dolls made of wood had hair of clay beads strung on twine. There were toy mice for toddlers. Made of wood, the toy mouse had a string fitted to its tail, so when a child pulled the string the tail went up and down. There were spinning tops molded of powered quartz and then glazed. A vigorous twist of the fingers, or a tug on a papyrus string wrapped around it, made the top spin. Board games were another popular sport. Senet, still played today, symbolized a struggle between forces of evil and the godly kingdom of Osiris; was this a forerunner of computer games? There was also a board game called "Snake," somewhat like Chinese checkers, except the board of squares was carved into the wooden back of a coiled serpent. The object was to move a stone (not a marble) around the squares on the snake's body and jump your partner's stone to reach the snake's head first.

a child, about four or five, its small body adorned with ivory bracelets and tiny lapis beads. Nearby were another thirty graves laid out in three neat rows. At the climax of his funeral, several lions were slain and placed in a separate burial pit. When Aha's body was lowered into a brick-lined burial chamber, a loyal group of courtiers and servants also took poison to join their king in the next world.

REPAIRS AND NEW CONSTRUCTION

When Ramses discovered that the tombs and temples of the former kings were in disastrous ruin, he commanded his workers to refurbish them: "His Majesty decreed that orders be given to the Chief of Works. He assigned soldiers, workmen, sculptors . . . every grade of craftsman to build his father's temple, and to restore what was ruined in the cemetery," wrote Kenneth A. Kitchen.

Work immediately began on his father's beautiful temple with its seven shrines. His most talented artists painted large murals of himself and Sethos, and scribes were instructed to oversee that all inscriptions were perfectly carved on the walls. Unlike Sethos's tomb, with its exquisite art and finish work, Ramses' monuments later appeared to have been much larger and showier. Perhaps he thought time was of the essence. There were more to be built.

VALLEY OF THE QUEENS

On the west bank of the Nile, across the river from Thebes, was the Valley of the Queens. Egyptologists estimated the necropolis contained about eight rock-cut tombs. It is staggering to think of all the men, materials, and years needed to build these magnificent edifices. Yet, tombs, temples, mastabas that were built over mummy chambers, and pyramids dotted the Egyptian landscape thousands of years before Ramses II.

In 2006, international officials were outraged when they discovered a French postman trying to sell bits of hair and cloth from the mummy of Ramses II *(above)*. Thought to be safe from grave robbers, the mummy has only left the Egyptian Museum in Cairo once, to be treated for a fungal infection in France.

When he was crowned king, not only did Ramses design plans for his own burial tomb, but for that of his first royal queen, Nefertari. Said to have been the most beautiful of his seven royal wives, scribes and artists were instructed to emblaze stunning scenes throughout her tomb. Nefertari appeared in a white linen gown, with six strands of amethysts around her neck, gold bracelets on her wrists, and her golden vulture crown with its two feathers artfully extending from the back. A small gold and turquoise cobra, threaded through her earlobe, marked her as royalty. Another frieze showed her worshipping the mummified body of Osiris. Equally stunning, another depicted her offering milk to the goddess Hathor. In one scene, the goddesses Nephthys and Isis watch hawk-like over the queen's mummy, portrayed as Osiris. To match Nefertari's radiance, Ramses ordered a pink granite sarcophagus. Befitting his royal wife, passages from the Book of the Dead emblazoned a wall, and his love for Nefertari was expressed: "For the one whose love shines. My love is unique—no one can rival her, for she is the most beautiful woman alive. Just by passing, she has stolen away my heart." Jimmy Dunn recaptured the endearment on www.touregypt.net/featurestories.

The Valley of the Queens was not only for wives of pharaohs, but for princes and princesses, and members of nobility. Egyptians called it Ta-Set-Neferu, "the Place of Children of the Pharaohs." Other family members entombed were Nebettawy, Ramses' daughter; Queen Meritamun, a daughter with Nefertari: Queen Bintanath, daughter of Ramses and Isetnofret; and several grandsons.

Long after Nefertari's death, another grandson was added to the sacred valley. Prince Amenhikhopeshef, son of Ramses III, was about nine years old when he died. Scenes showed his father presenting him to the gods, including Anubis, the jackal-headed god of the dead. A premature baby was also found in the tomb. Historians believe it to have belonged to his mother, who had miscarried upon learning of her other boy's death.

VALLEY OF THE KINGS

North of the Valley of the Queens, and also on the west bank of the Nile, was the rugged, sand-swept Valley of the Kings. It appeared as an irregular hollow, a desolate place among mountains of dry and barren land. Egyptians imagined the sun entered the underworld, realm of the dead, as it sank on the western horizon and chose this place hoping to join the setting sun on its evening journey toward resurrection the next morning. Each tomb consisted of a series of bays and corridors. Rock-hewed staircases reached down into a great golden hall for the pharaoh's sarcophagus. Walls inscribed sacred writings from the *Book of Him Who is in the Underworld,* the *Book of the Gates,* the *Sun's Journey in the Underworld,* the *Praising of Ra,* and the *Book of the Opening of the Mouth.* Texts were accompanied with illustrated ceremonies, spirits, and evil underworld gods. Myth foretold that the sun god Re sailed through the 12 regions of the underworld. Twelve caverns corresponded to the 12 hours of night, in which Re, for a short time, brought light and life. Several of the ceilings were a faded dark blue with faint yellow stars.

The first king buried in this valley was Thutmose I, father of Queen Hatshepsut, and Thutmose III, about 1501 B.C. For 500 years thereafter, all the rulers of Egypt were buried in the valley. The tombs have since been numbered. Ramses II is number KV7. After years of being looted and weathered, KV7 was empty and in despair. International plans are underway to restore the tomb. Ramses' mummy was later found and moved to the tomb of Sethos 1. It was then buried with other monarchs in the famous hidden cache of Deir el-Bahri. This was discovered in 1871, and the royal mummies were again moved to a museum in Thebes. The mummy is now on display in the Egyptian Museum in Cairo, and it is said to be the best preserved.

PIRAMSES, A NEW CAPITAL

Ramses had grandiose plans for Piramses ("Ramses' house"), his great royal palace (at modern-day Qantir). The old capital at Memphis, once the center of culture and theology, became the new seat of government. To make way for his delta palace and power base, he expanded Avaris, his place of birth. The city was strategically laid out near the road leading to the border fortress of Sile and the provinces of Palestine and Syria. Because of its location, Piramses became the most important international trade center and military base in all Egypt. Its regal splendor eventually rivaled ancient Memphis. Ramses often traveled between the delta and Upper Egypt, and as far as Aswan, to inspect his monument projects and discuss village concerns with local overlords. Despite the hundreds of workers, few accidents were reported and work appeared to exceed expectations.

By the second year of his reign, he was recognized for his architectural ability, strong management skills, and handsome royal appearance. Ramses was driven by his royal destiny and his demands for perfection in all phases of workmanship, and solid leadership gained him respect. Wherever he traveled, he radiated strength and gravitas.

CHAPTER

6

Master
Strategist

RAMSES' PLANS FOR THE GREAT TWIN TEMPLES BELOW ASWAN AT ABU
Simbel steadily progressed. All year long, brick makers and
limestone workers labored. Still, it would be 20 years before
the temples would be completed and dedicated to the gods
Amun-Re, Ptah, and Ra Harakhi, and to Ramses himself.
One huge project was the four colossal statues of the pharaoh
with the double crowns of Upper and Lower Egypt sculpted
to decorate the temple façade. Above the statues was a frieze
of 22 baboons, worshipers of the sun, and Harakhi holding a
hieroglyph in his right hand and a feather (Maat, goddess of
truth and justice) in his left. Ramses also ordered statues of
himself, Nefertari, the queen mother, and several princesses.

When Piramses was officially dedicated, the pharaoh ordered his royal chefs to prepare delicacies for the thousands who came to celebrate his new capital. Delta residents were enthusiastic about his lavish, blue-tiled buildings and called Piramses the Turquoise City. An artificial lake and stone buildings enhanced a verdant landscape of sycamores, palms, acacias, and flowering tamarisks. Showy and fragrant lotus blossoms floated in blue-green ponds highlighted with beds of papyrus and ornamental statues. Royals and the wealthy, eager to associate with the popular ruler, vied for land near the palace for their homes. Nefertari gave birth to her first daughter. Isetnofret and Ramses' young son showed keen interest in the kingship. The royal harem swelled with new babies. And Queen Mother Tuya appeared content to live with her son's growing family in the magnificent palace that sparkled with gold, turquoise, and lapis lazuli.

The annual harvest was plentiful, and the people were richly fed. The capital ran smoothly, despite trivial rivalry and gossip between the vassal lords and cabinet officials. Ramses' huge construction and restoration projects provided more work for peasants and craftspeople. Festive yearly celebrations and sacred events united the people, and prosperity and harmony appeared uppermost with many. With such imposing gifts from the gods, Ramses decided to make changes to his name. To "The Strong in Right is Re," a personal association with Re the sun god, he added *Usi-ma-re Stepenre*, "Chosen in Re." Strong in Right is Re Chosen by Re seemed to enhance his godly statue and public esteem.

UNRESOLVED AFFAIRS

Ramses now took on the old and unsolved problems of the monarchy. Whether or not he had been pleased with his father's mutual nonaggressive pact with the Hittites is uncertain. What is known is that Ramses had grown restless and now wanted

Ramses II enjoyed a sizable harem: He boasted 80 sons and 60 daughters. Some of his sons were trained for future kingship, while daughters took over their mothers' duties after retirement or death. The statue of Bint-Anath *(above)*, daughter of Ramses II, carved into a statue of the pharaoh at the Temple of Amun in Karnak, Egypt.

to conquer the intruders so that he could gain back all the Egyptian territories lost by previous pharaohs. To fund these campaigns and build and equip an army he needed gold. There were rich deposits in the eastern deserts around Nubia, but to mine the ore water was essential, and every past king had tried and failed. In the third year of his reign, Ramses formed a plan and summoned his court to discuss how to bring up a well.

"Now, one of these days . . . His Majesty was sitting on the electrum throne, wearing the head fillet and tall plumes . . . thinking about the desert lands where gold could be found, and meditating on plans for digging wells . . . Ramses' wishes were like magic. The court responded, 'You are like Re in all that you have done whatever your heart desires comes to pass. If you desire something overnight comes the dawn and it happen[s] immediately!'" according to Kenneth A. Kitchen.

Satisfied with this response, Ramses sent a survey to the Nubians. He commanded a well to appear on the route to Akuyati. As if Hapi had been waiting for Ramses' appeal, the god of the Nile responded. Overnight, water gushed forth at 12 cubits, a little more than 20 feet (6 meters) below ground. Not at all mystified by Ramses' close relationship, nor surprised by Hapi's immediate help, they were nevertheless elated. In honor of the new artesian well, Wadi Allaki, the court named it "the well, Ramses II is valiant of deeds."

In the fourth year of his reign, Ramses and his Egyptian army of charioteers, infantry of swords and shield bearers, and Sea People in his captivity, set sail for Syria. They journeyed northward along the Phoenician coast. Canaan (Palestine and Phoenicia), Amurru, and Syria formed a vast bubble zone between the warring empires. When they reached Tyra, they advanced overland and eastward to attack Amurru (site of modern-day Lebanon) in the vicinity of Qadesh. Surprised by the unexpected Egyptian assault, Hittite ally and overlord Prince Benteshina was unable to defend Amurru. To prevent any further loss of territory, he surrendered the city. Benteshina became a tribute-paying vassal of Egypt. Confident with his effortless conquest, many prisoners, and much Hittite booty, Ramses planned to conquer the Hittites at Qadesh the following year. Upon their return to Piramses, the victorious battle was carved on the walls of the major temples.

THE BATTLE OF QADESH

Thinking the Hittite too frightened to confront the formidable Egyptian army, Ramses mounted his first major campaign. Day and night the armory workshops produced shields, spears, and battleaxes. Thousands of wooden chariots rolled out of carpentry sheds. He ordered countless arrows and bows, finger guards, and wrist protectors made of animal gut. Archers practiced their marksmanship, taking orders by trumpet. Combat forces were instructed in hand-to-hand warfare, and riders and their horses received extensive military training. Magnificent ships were built in naval yards stretched along riverbanks. Capable of long journeys in deep and churning seas, Ramses demanded the ships be made of highly prized cedar of Lebanon.

With massive preparations completed, Ramses boarded his golden barge fully ready to wage war against his bitter rival. The Egyptian fleet sailed from Piramses with wild animals, horses, ancillary elements, and 20,000 men and charioteers. They were divided into forces of 5,000 men each, and they marched under the standards of Egypt's four greatest gods: Amun, Re, Ptah, and Seth.

Unbeknownst to Ramses, the Hittite king, Muwatallis, was not to be fooled again. During the past year he had brought together a formidable army. Sir Alan Gardiner, in *The Kadesh Inscriptions of Ramesses II*, described the army as "all the foreign lands as far as the end of the sea. . . . They covered the mountains and the valleys and were like locusts in their multitude."

Nineteen thousand men and 2,500 chariots. He vowed that when Ramses and his army returned, the Hittite army would crush them.

Overconfident and self-assured with his huge and well-equipped army, and with misleading information from his scouts, Ramses unknowingly marched toward an ambush. Behind him was his military staff, several of his young sons, members of the royal family, household butlers, and a body-guard who was also probably one of his sons.

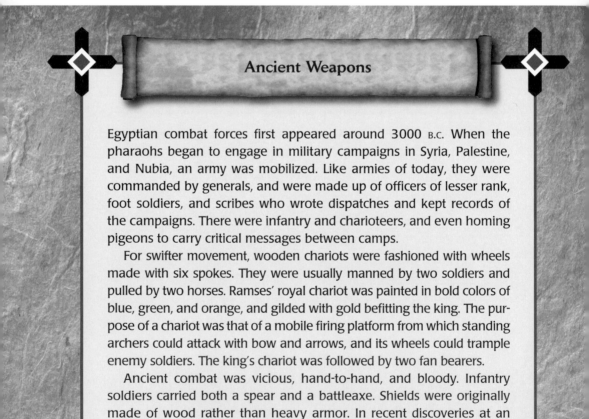

Ancient Weapons

Egyptian combat forces first appeared around 3000 B.C. When the pharaohs began to engage in military campaigns in Syria, Palestine, and Nubia, an army was mobilized. Like armies of today, they were commanded by generals, and were made up of officers of lesser rank, foot soldiers, and scribes who wrote dispatches and kept records of the campaigns. There were infantry and charioteers, and even homing pigeons to carry critical messages between camps.

For swifter movement, wooden chariots were fashioned with wheels made with six spokes. They were usually manned by two soldiers and pulled by two horses. Ramses' royal chariot was painted in bold colors of blue, green, and orange, and gilded with gold befitting the king. The purpose of a chariot was that of a mobile firing platform from which standing archers could attack with bow and arrows, and its wheels could trample enemy soldiers. The king's chariot was followed by two fan bearers.

Ancient combat was vicious, hand-to-hand, and bloody. Infantry soldiers carried both a spear and a battleaxe. Shields were originally made of wood rather than heavy armor. In recent discoveries at an

Unseen, the Hittite army allowed Ramses and his first division to pass. When their backs were against the enemy, the huge army of charioteers that Muwatallis had mustered swooped down and destroyed the second division. The clang of shields, the thunder of thrashing horses, and the zing of arrows pierced the rock-strewn hills. In the rear, the third division was still crossing the Orontes River. In swift advance, the Hittites turned to crush Ramses. So great was the grisly onslaught of enemy warriors that the pharaoh's army weakened and attempted to

ancient Egyptian armory workshop, it appeared that later craftsmen used stone molds to produce Hittite-style shields for the army.

There were numerous styles of flint heads inserted into the tips of reed shaft arrows. Some were horseshoe shaped and were designed to wound the enemy; others were sharp and triangular and were meant to kill the victim outright. The first arrowheads were made of flint or hardwood. Later, bronze was used.

Egyptian daggers looked frightening and were certainly deadly weapons. Long, tapered copper blades were decorated with narrow stripes with a wide handle. An ivory or bone pommel at the top of the dagger was made to fit into the palm of a hand. Daggers were held in the belt of a kilt or in a wooden sheath overlaid with gold. There were various sizes and lengths of swords with handles smoother than daggers and much longer blades. Foot soldiers carried lances and javelins.

After "stinging the enemy," a phrase referring to distinguishing oneself in battle, a soldier was awarded a gold medal shaped like a fly and also received other gifts of gratitude.

desert. In a moment of decision, Ramses turned for help from Amun.

> I found Amun came when I called to him,
> He gave me his hand and I rejoiced.
> He called from behind as if nearby:
> "Forward, I am with you,
> I, your father, my hand is with you,
> I prevail over a hundred thousand men,
> I am lord of victory, lover of valour!"
>
> —Sir Alan Gardiner

Instilled with Amun's inspired strength, Ramses leaped into his golden chariot and tied the reins around his waist to leave his hands free. He seized his weapons, rose up in his chariot, belted his armor, and with his pet lion and great horses, charged at great speed; six times did he attack the fray. Later it was inscribed that Ramses single-handedly charged the enemy forces: "The 2,500 spans of chariotry, in whose midst I was, became heaps of corpses before my horses," as excerpted from the walls of the Ramesseum.

Seeing Ramses courageously strike back at the enemy, his troops rallied the charge and joined in hot pursuit. Help arrived with the third division and then the fourth division at sunset. By nightfall, Ramses' charioteers and warriors had slaughtered thousands of Hittites and driven as many into the river. To tally the number of enemy dead, Ramses' generals ordered one hand per corpse be taken.

Planning to completely wipe out the Hittite enemy the next morning, Ramses was surprised when word came from King Muwatallis seeking a truce. Ramses refused to make a peace agreement and the battle ended in a stalemate. As it was, the Hittite had previously been threatened by the Assyrians. Ramses was forced to deal with Libyan insurgents. A sealed agreement would have to wait.

Outnumbered and under siege, Ramses II led the Egyptian army against the Hittites at the battle of Qadash. With the arrival of reinforcements, the young pharaoh was able to defeat his enemy. Documented on a stone tablet *(above)*, a peace pact was later forged by both kingdoms.

According to NationMaster, The Battle of Qadesh (Tell Nabi Mend) is one of the most famous armed conflicts of antiquity. Much of the battle action was due to Ramses himself. Since the nineteenth century, the temple complex Ramesseum at Luxor, between Gurnah and the desert, has been known by his name. Ramses commissioned scribes and artists to detail his bravery and describe his epic battle and great success. Walls and pylon façades showed Ramses' triumphant charge. Literary and pictorial panels dramatized scenes of the war and the rout of the Hittites. His pet lion was depicted at his side. A closer look revealed more lions attacking enemy soldiers. At least 14 of Ramses' young sons participated in some part of the action. According to Sir Alan Gardiner, "The account of the Hittite war is a unique phenomenon of Egyptian literature."

Names of Ramses' sons and daughters appear elsewhere in the tomb. The ancient Greek historian Diodorus Siculo "marveled at Pharaohs gigantic and famous temple and its accounts of the battle of Qadesh." Critical historians, such as Nicolas Grimal, claim the Ramses victory "was nothing of the sort. He had simply managed to rescue his army." Elizabeth Payne wrote, "But, in truth the Battle of Qadesh was no victory at all. Ramses had walked into a trap, had lost numbers of his army, had failed to capture Qadeah—and had neither defeated the Hittites decisively, nor driven them north into their own lands again."

Controversy over the outcome of the battle continued through the ages. Poets referred to Ramses II as an arrogant tyrant and a vicious warrior who ruled Egypt with an iron hand, slew thousands of his enemies, and built gigantic stone statues of himself. In 1881, Percy Bysshe Shelley published *Ozymandias*, generally believed to refer to Ramses the Great.

Ozymandias

I met a traveler from an antique land
Who said: Two vast and trunkless legs of stone
Stand in the desert. Near them on the sand,

Half sunk, a shatter'd visage lies, whose frown
And wrinkled lip and sneer of cold command
Tell that its sculptor well those passions read
Which yet survive, stamp'd on these lifeless things.
The hand that mock'd them and the heart that fed.
And on the pedestal these words appear:
"My name is Ozymandias, king of kings:
Look on my works, ye mighty, and despair!"
Nothing beside remains: round the decay
Of that colossal wreck, boundless and bare,
The lone and level sands stretch far away.

The sonnet represents a transliteration into Greek of a part of Ramses' throne name, Usi-ma-re Stepenre. It paraphrases the inscription on the base of a fallen colossus statue of Ramses at Ramesseum. Composed by Diodorus Siculus it reads, "King of Kings am I, Osymandias. If anyone would know how great I am and where I lie, let him surpass one of my works."

Ironically, after the greatest battle in ancient history, Ramses' army returned to Piramses, and Muwatallis replaced Benteshina. The land Ramses had claimed for Egypt returned to the Hittites.

7

Fields of Endeavor

AFTER THE BATTLE OF QADESH, RAMSES CONTINUED TO CAMPAIGN EACH year against the Hittites in Syria and Palestine. His Egyptian army captured towns that were recaptured by the Hittites, and then taken again by the Egyptians. Ramses briefly captured the cities of Tunip, where no Egyptian soldier had been in 120 years. In the eighth and ninth years of his reign, he once again captured Qadesh. But over the years both armies had fought to a standstill. Tens of thousands of soldiers and civilians died or suffered injuries, and villages and towns were destroyed and rebuilt. In between wars on the Syrian front, Ramses campaigned south of the first cataract into Nubia. Gold and the pharaoh's taxes provoked the various viceroys, and minor skirmishes erupted. Weary of reoccurring revolts, Ramses decided to quell the problem once and for all. Using his large and seasoned army, the campaign was swift and forceful. Ramses' soldiers victoriously returned home with 7,000 prisoners and much booty. Nubia was never to revolt again.

MEDICINE AND SURGERY

There were, of course, many soldiers who did not die from their battle wounds. Many suffered pain and infection, and there were injuries in the brickfields and workshops. Women and children died from accidents and a variety of diseases, or often died during childbirth. There were no pharmacies or patent medicines 3,500 years ago. There were, however, many ointments, tonics, creams, infusions, and poultices.

Imhotep was a skilled physician who later was considered the Egyptian god of healing. Ancient Egypt also gave the world one of its first medical texts, the Papyrus Ebers, named for the German Egyptologist Georg Ebers. He purchased it in 1873 from an Arab who claimed to have found it in a necropolis outside Thebes. The papyrus is believed to have been written in the sixteenth century B.C. It contained some 800 recipes and listed over 700 drugs, including aloe, wormwood, peppermint, henbane, myrrh, hemp, dogbane, castor oil, and mandrake. The papyrus offered a suggestion for treatment for diabetes.

The Papyrus Ebers described the position of the heart precisely and illustrated some of its disorders. The writer also knew that the blood supply ran from the heart to all the organs. According to Dr. Sameh M. Arab, professor of cardiology at Alexandria University in Cairo, "This knowledge could only have been gained through experience." Dr. Arab also pointed out that the process of examination used today follows similar steps used by ancient physicians.

In the eighth century B.C., the Greek poet Homer recognized Egyptian ancient medicine and wrote, "In Egypt, the men are more skilled in medicine than any human kind." And according to Herodotus, King Cyrus of Persia requested Ahmose II of the Twenty-sixth Dynasty to send him the most skillful of all Egyptian eye doctors. The Kahun Gynecology Papyrus dates back to 1825 B.C. and described methods of diagnosing pregnancy and telling the sex of a fetus, toothache, diseases of women, and feminine drugs and pastes, as stated on the Web site The History of Herodotus.

The Edwin Smith Papyrus was chiefly concerned with surgery. It described 48 surgical cases of the head, neck, shoulders, breast, and chest. It included vast knowledge of treating fractures that could only have been acquired at a site where accidents occurred, such as when building of the pyramids.

Mud or moldy bread was placed over sores or wounds to keep them from becoming infected. Thousands of years later, medical scientists discovered that mud and mold contain certain microorganisms, bacteria, and fungi that produce one class of antibiotic drugs.

Garlic bulbs were said to bring good health, ward off diseases, and kill intestinal parasitic worms. Herodotus wrote that nine tons of gold was spent on onions to feed the pyramid builders and to use as an external antiseptic and for pain relief.

Mustard has been recognized as medicine since time immemorial. Its name, *Sinapis*, is of Egyptian origin. Ground seeds mixed with water were used as a laxative and to relieve indigestion. Homemade plasters from the seed were applied to sore muscles. The oil of mustard was used for ingredients in ointments.

Five thousand years ago, Egyptians used dill for seasoning foods, soothing infant colic, scenting perfume, treating kidney complaints, and digestive disorders in older children. Rosemary is said to have strengthened the memory, made a fine cup of tea, flavored meat dishes, and rid the body of intestinal gas.

Celebrating his new peace agreement with the Hittites, as well as his victory at Qadash, Ramses II memorialized himself at his Great Temple at Abu Simbel. Carved out of stone, the giant statues of Ramses II *(above)* are more than 20 meters high.

Flax, grown for meal and cloth, was also used for salves, relief of coughs, colds, constipation, and poultices for boils and burns.

During campaigns in foreign lands, soldiers gathered seeds and roots. Upon returning home they planted them in their gardens and farms, or they were used for remedies concocted by Egyptian alchemists.

Visible wounds and injuries were treated by various methods according to the papyruses, noted Dr. Arab, while internal diseases were thought to be due to an occult force attributed to evil gods, a divine punishment, or magical procedure.

Sacred Rituals

Egyptian priests were powerful and were believed to have an intimate relationship with the gods as well as the pharaohs; their methods were unquestioned. High priests were responsible for the numerous secret rituals that took place in the temples' sanctuaries. They held titles to indicate their rank, such as God's Servant . Lower-level priests were called Pure Ones or God's Fathers. They served on a rotating system and were responsible for maintaining temple property and keeping administrative records.

Sacred rituals began with a procession of bald priests—their heads shaved to ensure cleanliness—entering the secret rooms, carrying incenses and oil lamps, and scattering purified water from the temple's sacred lake. Water mixed with natron was carried in sacred buckets decorated with carved images of gods or crescents and full moons worshiped by baboons. The water was used to pour over an offering for ritual washing before and after eating at temple festivals or religious rituals. The tray to hold the incense was shaped like an outstretched arm with a flat hand that held a cup of fragrances. There were bronze incense burners, too, that allowed the aroma to rise with the smoke. The pleasing scents drifted in the temple's cool air to attract the attention of the gods and to purify the atmosphere. Another priest might carry a standard, such as a supporting pole inscribed with the emblem of papyrus plants topped with the falcon god, Horus. Horus wore the combined crowns of Upper and Lower Egypt that identified him with the king.

Doctors, however, were aware that the brain was the seat of body control, and many of the medical procedures and treatments today can be traced to the knowledge of ancient remedies and cures.

As priests approached a shrine, they might have chanted, "I am a pure one." Then carefully they broke the clay seal on the door. Inside was revealed a golden statue of a god. Before making an offering of food, they decorated the statue with semiprecious gems. As they left, one priest silently swept the floor so no crumbs would leave a trace of their presence.

Deniu-en-Khons was a priestess who also made offerings to the gods. She might have offered a mirror, its face carved with the head of Hathor with a background of religious symbols, or a palace scene with the royal queen sitting on her throne. Hathor's head adorned the ivory handle. The beautifully painted mirrors and cosmetic pallets were placed in temples for the gods' use. Other objects offered may have included a bronze plaque showing a priest offering loaves of bread and a delicately crafted vase of liquid. At the front of the plaque was a hole where the holy liquid could drain away.

There were elaborate morning and evening hymns to awake or take leave of the gods and books of spells and recitations for special rites. Inscribed with the sacred scenes were greetings by priests or the temple choir; such religious words of praise have come down through the ages.

Certain sacred animals were attributed to the gods, such as the ibis and baboon for Thoth, god of wisdom and magic; the cat of Bast; the ram of Khnum; Sobek the crocodile, or Horus the falcon-headed god of day. The frog-headed Heqet was the goddess of birth. During Ramses' long reign, there were sacred beasts like Apis, the bull; Ptah at Memphis; and the Mnevis bull at Heliopolis. Such were the sacred and mystical beliefs of ancient Egyptians.

AWESOME ABU SIMBEL

Ramses' celebration of victory over the Hittites had been dramatized in art compositions and poetic narrative. Temple inscriptions recounted his heroics. Three times was his story told at the Luxor temple on pylon façades, the exterior of courts, and its interiors. When it was all said and done, Ramses, tireless and ambitious, turned to yet a new project. This time his eyes were attracted south to Nubia for his memorial temple. Two great bluffs of pinkish sandstone rose out of the west bank of the Nile north of Aksha. Here, two huge sanctuaries were to be carved out of the rock 160 feet (48.7 m) into the mountain. The four colossal figures of the pharaoh, over 65 feet (19.8 m) high, were to announce the entrance to the Great Temple of Ramses II.

A few hundred yards away, cut into the northern bluff, was another splendid temple dedicated to the goddess Hathor for Queen Nefertari. It was marked by six giant statues of Ramses and Nefertari with smaller statues of their children. A flight of steps cut into the rock gave access to the antechamber, which held wall paintings based on the Book of the Dead. Like her monument in the Valley of the Queens, it had a dark blue ceiling that gave the appearance of heaven sprinkled with a myriad of golden five-pointed stars. Beneath was the burial chamber with more wall art from the Book of the Dead concerning the gates and opening to the kingdom of Osiris. Inscribed was a magic chant the deceased had to utter to pass through the doors.

More work was done on the Hypostyle Hall at Karnak with the addition of a forest of pillars so big around that 100 men could stand atop each. A flock of geese inhabited the sacred lake. During festivals, images of the gods on their golden barges sailed across the clear blue water. Ramses built temple after temple, often with stones from other pharaohs' tombs, which he pulled down and carted away for his own use. He challenged superstition and made off with marble and granite blocks from Akhenaton's crumbing City of the Horizon to build a temple across the river.

In the nineteenth year of his reign, as if enough was enough or he was weary of twenty some years of fighting, Ramses decided to conclude a peace agreement with the new Hittite king, Hattusil III.

PRELUDE TO PEACE

His old enemy, Muwatallis, had died. For seven years, Urhi-Teshub, Muwatallis's son by a concubine, reigned as the Hittite great king. In the north, his uncle Hattusil, a high priest and local king, had more ambitious ideas. After a winning battle against Urhi-Teshub, Hattusil became king. He promoted a better understanding with neighboring countries, all except Egypt. In the meantime, rather than kill his nephew, King Hattusil had him banished to north Syria or the seacoast. But Urhi-Teshub slipped away to Egypt.

Angry that he had been outsmarted by his nephew, who was evidently accepted by the Egyptians, Hattusil felt threatened. Suppose Ramses backed Urhi-Teshub as legitimate heir to the Hittite throne? Hattusil, now allied with Babylon, demanded the young man's return. Ramses refused. Both sides raised their battle flags and mobilized for war.

Their threats against each other, however, were complicated by outside forces. Hanigalbat's army was overwhelmed by the Assyrian army and they lost. Assyria now controlled all the land along the Euphrates River and bordered the Syrian province. Hattusil was now faced with foes in the east and south. Who should he assault first and could he fight on several fronts at once?

Hattusil must have given his predictiment considerable forethought. Finally he decided to slowly and discreetly seek out peace negotiations with Egypt. For many months, envoys journeyed back and forth between the two capitals, from Anatolia to the stunning new capital of Piramses, refining terms and intentions. At last a peace treaty seemed ready for signing.

8

The
Peace Treaty

THE TREATY BETWEEN THE EGYPTIANS AND THE HITTITES WAS THE earliest recorded peace treaty in ancient history. Diplomatic negotiations lasted over two years as envoys traveled between the two countries—a one-month journey each way. It ended the war with Syria and marked a clear line of demarcation between the Egyptian and Syrian territories. Egypt guaranteed the Hittites the right to use their Phoenician harbors, the ancient coastal plains of what is now Lebanon. The Hittites agreed to allow Egyptians free passage, without interference, to the north as far as Ugarit, the ancient Syrian capital on the Mediterranean coast.

Signed and confirmed by each party in 1259 B.C., today it is considered of such importance in the field of international relations that a reproduction hangs in the United Nations head-quarters. Acknowledged by Ramses II, king of Egypt, and Hattusil III, the Hittite emperor, it was the first state-to-state treaty. The Egyptian version was reported on two steles, one at the Karnak temple of Amun and the other at the Ramesseum. The treaty included extradition clauses for political opponents and provided the basis for a lasting peace. Throughout the remainder of Ramses' 67 years of kingship, the two countries had no further conflict with one another. Personal links were forged between the two royal families, traced through 26 letters sent to Hattusil and 13 sent to his wife, Pudukhepa. Parallel versions of the treaty were kept in each capital, one transcribed in Egyptian hieroglyphics, the other in Akkadian, using cuneiform script. Both versions survive.

The majority of the text is identical except the Hittite version claimed the Egyptians came suing for peace. The Egyptian version claimed the reverse. The treaty was presented to the Egyptians in the form of a silver plaque. The treaty contained 18 articles: first for peace, then that of their countries' respective gods who also demanded peace, and a simple declaration to end hostilities. Egypt's acceptance ended the war in Syria but meant there would be no chance to restore Qadesh and Amurru. In return for this sacrifice, the dispute between the two countries ended with a clear line of demarcation between Egyptian and Syrian territories. This privilege had been lost for more than a century. The agreement contained a mutual-assistance pact in the event that one of the empires should be attacked by a third party, or in the event of internal strife. Additional articles pertained to the repatriation of refugees and provisos that they should not be harmed; this could be considered as the first extradition treaty. There were also threats of retribution, should the treaty be broken. Following are excerpts from the peace treaty, as told in *Peace Treaty Between Egypt and the Hittite*, by Dr. Sameh M. Arab:

"Reamasesa, the great king, the king of the country of Egypt, shall never attack the country of Hatti to take possession of a part (of this country). And Hattusili, the great king, the king of the country of Hatti, shall never attack the country of Egypt to take possession of a part (of that country)."

"If a foreign enemy marches against the country of Hatti and if Hattusili, the king of the country of Hatti, sends me this message: 'Come to my help against him,' Reamasesa, the great king, the king of the Egyptian country, has to send his troops and his chariots to kill this enemy and to give satisfaction to the country of Hatti."

To avoid any further dispute, if a refugee should flee to the other country, ten articles were dedicated to their extradition. Here is one:

"If a great person flees from the country of Hatti and if he comes to Reamasesa, the great king, king of the country of Egypt, then Reamasesa, the great king, the king of the country of Egypt, has to take hold of him and deliver him into hands of Hattusili, the great king, the king of the country of Hatti."

Both sides agreed that fugitives were to be treated with dignity and returned without being punished:

"If a man flees from the country of Hatti, or two men, or three men, and if they come to Reamasesa, the Great King, the king of the country of Egypt, his brother, then Reamasesa, the Great King, the king of the country of Egypt, has to take hold of them and to order them to be taken to Hattusili, his brother, since they are brothers. As for their crime, it should not be imputed; their language and their eyes are not to be pulled out; their ears and their feet are not to be cut off; their houses with their wives and their children are not to be destroyed."

In the last two articles, the 1,000 gods of either land were invoked as witnesses and guarantors of the peace. Only some of the gods were named, including Ra, the great god of Egypt, and Teshub, the storm and weather god of the Hittites. As soon as the treaty became effective, greetings were exchanged between the two courts, particularly from the two queens, Nefertari of Egypt and Pudukhepa, the Hittite queen. Nefertari wrote, as

In an attempt to establish peace between their two kingdoms, Ramses II and King Hattusil III of the Hittite kingdom corresponded regularly by letters carved into stone tablets *(above)*. The two finalized the peace treaty after Ramses II married one of Hattusil's daughters.

told by Dr. Sameh M. Arab in *Peace Treaty Between Egypt and the Hittite*:

> I hear, my sister that you have written to ask after my peace
> and the relations of good peace and fraternity that exists

between the Great King of Egypt and the Great King of Hatti, his brother. Ra and Teshub will deal with this so you can raise your look, may Ra assure the peace and strengthen the good fraternity between the Great King of Egypt and the Great King of Hatti, his brother, for ever.

OTHER PEACE TREATIES

Numerous peace treaties have been attempted and signed since then. The Treaty of Paris (1815) was signed after Napoleon's defeat at the Battle of Waterloo. The Treaty of Versailles (1919) formally ended the First World War. The latter treaty is possibly the most notorious of peace treaties in that some historians blamed it for the rise of National Socialism in Germany and the eventual outbreak of the Second World War. Others argued that the cause was reasonable in that it reflected the harsh terms Germany had negotiated with Russia with the Treaty of Brest-Litovsk. Germany was forced to pay the victors and had to accept sole responsibility for starting the war, and the harsh restrictions on German rearmament all listed in the treaty caused further massive resentment in Germany. The debate over whether the Treaty of Versailles can be blamed for starting another war or not shows the difficulties involved in making peace agreements. This treaty created the League of Nations and was a major goal of United States President Woodrow Wilson. It was signed by the "Big Three" nations: the United States, France, and Great Britain.

Treaties became binding in international laws and the rules laid down in the Vienna Convention of the Law of Treaties, 1969. Numerous issues can be included in a peace treaty, and its content usually depends heavily on the nature of the conflict being concluded. Some might be formal designations of borders, such as the Treaty of Versailles; processes for resolving future disputes; determinations of access to and apportioning of natural resources; deciding status of prisoners and refugees; settling existing debts and ownership claims as with the Ramses/

Hittite treaty; defining proscribed behavior; or reapplication of existing treaties.

There was no peace treaty at the conclusion of the U.S. Civil War since the losing side surrendered and its government

The Exodus

Was Ramses the Great pharaoh of the Exodus? The biblical Exodus of the Jews from Egypt is generally thought to date from the reign of Ramses II, though no such episode appears in Egyptian records or is linked to the expulsion of the Hyksos by Ahmose.

The Exodus was the great deliverance extended to the Israelites "... on the very day the Lord brought the people of Israel out of the land of Egypt by their hosts," Exodus 12:51.

"There is no surviving Egyptian source that described the Exodus. This is not surprising," commented Nicolas Grimal, "given that the Egyptians had no reason to attach any importance to the Hebrews."

Documents place the people known as Apiru in Egyptian records at the time of Tuthmose III. During Ramses' reign, the Apiru were employed in the transportation of stone listed in Leiden Papyrus 348; they were further mentioned in Papyrus Harris I. As brick makers they were mentioned in the neighborhood of the royal harem at Medinet el-Ghurob in the Fayum. In the reign of Ramses IV, about 800 worked in the quarries of Wadi Hammamat.

"One document that could provide evidence of a newly formed kingdom of Israel is a stele, dated to the fifth year of Merneptah's reign," as told in *New Unger's Bible Dictionary*. "Here the name Israel appears (KRI IV, 12–19). There are two further historical records: the journey of the Chosen People in the desert, which lasted forty years, and the capture of Jericho, which occurred after the death of Moses. The fall of

collapsed. The Korean War was an example of a war that was suspended with a cease-fire but was never closed with a treaty.

The Treaty of Tordesillas (1494), between Spain and Portugal, is an interesting document in that it revolved around meridi-

Jericho sets the day of 1250 B.C. So the Exodus may have taken place in the early part of the thirteenth century B.C."

Various scholars have placed Moses in close relationship with Pharaoh Ramses II and as the son of Queen Hatshepsut, who later assumed the Egyptian throne. Moses received his Egyptian education (Acts 7:22) to represent his community in the government. His education at the court (Exodus 2:10– 11) may be interpreted as he benefited from the education provided to future Egyptian state employees. Thus, he would have been with his own people during the reign of Sethos I, the time fortifications were built in the eastern delta and foundations were built for the future city of Piramses (Exodus 1:11). "Therefore they set taskmasters over them to afflict them with heavy burdens; and they built for Pharaoh store-cities, Pithom and Raam'ses."

"It is often speculated that Jewish captives worked on the construction of Piramses," wrote Bernadette Menu. Was this biblical spelling meant to be Piramses?

Moses's murder of the guard, his flight to the land of Midian, his marriage, his acceptance of God's revelation, the encounter with the Burning Bush, and his return to Egypt take the dates to the first years of Ramses II's reign. The book of Exodus has lengthy descriptive dialogue between Moses and a pharaoh.

If one is to set aside the Old Testament's chronological dates, the Exodus could be placed around 1290 B.C. rather than 1441 B.C. This would suggest the pharaoh of the Exodus was Ramses II.

Nefertari, the tireless partner of Ramses II, managed his harem and played a minor role in developing the peace agreement with the Hittite kingdom. In appreciation of her abilities, Ramses II built her a smaller, lavish temple at Abu Simbel. This Ninteenth-Dynasty statue of the two stands as testament to their partnership.

ans. Just months after Christopher Columbus returned to Europe from his maiden voyage to the New World, the Spanish-born Pope Alexander VI gave Spain a head start in the quest for domination over newly discovered regions of the world. He decreed that all lands discovered west of a meridian 100 leagues (one league is 3 miles or 4.8 km) west of the Cape Verde Islands would belong to Spain. New lands discovered east of that line would belong to Portugal. He further specified that all lands already under the control of a "Christian prince" would remain under that same control. You can imagine the results of this treaty.

King John II of Portugal negotiated with King Ferdinand and Queen Isabella of Spain to move the line to the west; the pope's line extended all around the globe limiting Spanish influence in Asia. On June 7, 1494, Spain and Portugal signed a treaty to move the line 270 leagues, to 370 leagues west of Cape Verde. The new line (located at approximately 46° 37') gave Portugal claim to South America and provided the country automatic control over most of the Indian Ocean. Due to problems determining longitude, it was several hundred years before the line could be accurately determined. Portugal and Spain kept to their sides of the line. Portugal ended up colonizing Brazil, India, and Macau in Asia.

CONCLUSION OF THE RAMSES/HITTITE PEACE TREATY

Peace endured during the next 46 regal years of Ramses' kingship. When the king of Mira in Asia Minor attempted to form a coalition with Egypt against the Hittites, Ramses refused saying, "Today there is fraternity between the Great King of Egypt and the King of Hatti, between Ra and Teshub." The treaty was respected until the fall of the Hittite Empire about 1150 B.C.

Bernadette Menu observed, "The pharaoh thus magnificently fulfilled his fundamental obligations as son and heir to the gods. An era of peace and prosperity, even of opulence, followed the war, and Egypt experienced decades of well-being, until the death of Ramses II."

9

Nightfall

DESPITE THE READINESS OF BOTH EMPIRES TO ABIDE BY THE PEACE TREATY, tension persisted for 10 years after the agreement because the Hittite prince, Urhi-Teshub, remained in political asylum in Egypt. King Hattusil repeatedly requested his surrender, and Ramses refused, applying the treaty in retrospect. Animosity, however, did not deter communications between the two rulers, or Ramses and his Egyptian army from celebrating his great victory. All over the country he was called Ramses the Great!

A spectacular feast welcomed him home: trays of honey cakes, dried fish, meats, bowls of figs and pomegranates, royal delicacies prepared for the thousands who came to celebrate his triumph. Refreshments were sent to distant villages so everyone could celebrate with the pharaoh and his gods. Acrobats,

harem dancers, musicians with their wild assortment of instru-
ments, colorful flag bearers, and bouquets of flowers showered
the city with jubilance and credulous acclaim. In temples, the
statues of the gods were washed, anointed, perfumed, dressed,
and offered food, water, and more flowers. Ramses' horses, Victory at Thebes and Mut Is Pleased, used to pull his chariot in
the Battle of Qadesh, were exalted in the tomb art of Rekhmira,
a vizier under King Thutmose III. Goldsmiths embellished the
king's handsome ring with two miniature gold horses. It was
a historic time in ancient Egypt, with inscribed and illustrated
compositions on numerous monuments, steles, and papyruses.

Thirty-five hundred years later, Christian Jacq elegantly
wrote of the pharaoh, "His titles proclaimed him the sun; the
powerful bull, the protector of Egypt and conqueror of foreign
lands, the king of resounding victories, the chosen son of divine
light. He was Ramses. In a golden crown, wearing silver armor
and a gold-trimmed kilt, holding a bow in his left hand and
a sword in his right, he stood erect on the platform of a lily-
trimmed chariot . . . the Nubian lion with his blazing mane, had
kept pace with the horses. Ramses' beauty combined both magic
and radiance. He was the ultimate expression of what a pharaoh
should be."

Year after year, the empire of Ramses the Great passed peace-
fully with more sons and daughters, and it was unsurpassed in
courtly opulence. After the Battle of Qadesh, he proclaimed
benefits for soldiers and artisans, and pensions for soldiers' wid-
ows. Ramses celebrated the annual floods of the Nile, the source
of all life, and mandated sacrifices to the gods of oxen, sheep,
and geese. Grand titles and public appearances proclaimed his
prominence. He reduced the responsibilities of the high priests,
who had gained much power over the years, and placed himself
as principal minister of all Egyptian divinities. A small bronze
statuette found in a tomb showed Ramses holding the heka
scepter, similar to a shepherd's crook. It was a symbol of the
inalienable and absolute sovereignty of a king.

THE SED FESTIVAL

The elaborate Sed Festival honored the god Maat, who gave Ramses the ability to carry on the creative work of the gods who had given him life and power. Traditionally, the New Year's ceremonies confirmed the king's royal power between himself and the people of Egypt, and enabled him to maintain and nourish the life forces that made the land fertile and part of the great cycles of the universe. The gods responded by granting him the favors that enabled him to bring Maat to the land.

Ramses' first Sed Festival was held in the thirteenth year of his reign. As if by godly intervention, that year the river filled the valley with life-giving powers that rejuvenated the soil and produced a bountiful harvest.

RAMSES' ROYAL FAMILY

In the twenty-second year of his reign, royal Queen Mother Tuya passed into her afterlife. Ramses had prepared a beautiful tomb for her in the Valley of the Queens. An impressive and sacred ceremony recognized her many years as devoted royal wife and endearing royal mother.

Grounded in her husband's rule while Ramses was away from the capital, his chief consort, Queen Nefertari, held his exalted position. In the grand audience chamber she conducted court, heard grievances, and governed his correspondences. She supervised her large royal household and a girls' school where young women received instructions in art, weaving, and music. Elegant and composed, Nefertari stood alongside Ramses at public and state ceremonies. Two of his sisters, Tia, and his younger sister, Hentmire, assumed their places as official wives of the king, as did two other sisters.

Ramses had brought all of Egypt's male children, born on the same day as he, together. He assigned them guardians with

Known as the horse-ring, this beautiful gold ring belonged to Ramses II. Goldsmiths embellished the king's ring with twin horses after he completed the peace treaty.

identical training and education for each. His principal was that with close companionship they would be the most loyal, and as fellow combatants in wars, the most brave. The king also provided for their every need and demanded they run 20 miles (32.18 km) before they had anything to eat. His theory was that when they reached manhood each would be robust and

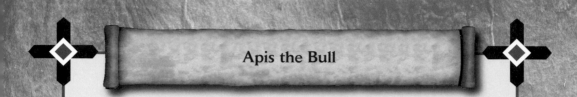

Apis the Bull

Animal cults were very important during the declining centuries of pharaonic Egypt. Apis, the sacred bull of Memphis, believed to be the animal form of the beautiful soul of the god Ptah, was no exception: "And whereas he bestowed many gifts upon Apis and Mnevi (the sacred bull of Heliopolis) and upon the other sacred animals in Egypt, because he was much more considerate than the kings before him of all that belonged to the gods; and for their burials he gave what was suitable lavishly and splendidly, and what was regularly paid to their special shrines, with sacrifices and festivals and other customary observances; and he maintained the honours of the temples and of Egypt according to the laws; and he adorned the temple of Apis with rich work, spending upon it gold and silver and precious stones, no small amount."

Bulls were carefully selected and lived long, pampered lives. When a sacred bull died, he was given an elaborate ceremony conducted by a current vizier. Gifts such as amulets and shabit figures were presented by priests and high officials. For each burial, the mummified body of the dead bull was hauled down a sloping ramp to a burial chamber cut into the rock at the Saqqara burial grounds in Memphis. Nearby tombs of previous bulls were each crowned with a little chapel. On one tomb panel, Ramses and Prince Khaemwaset were shown in reverence before Apis.

On the death of a bull, a new bull with similar markings had to be found and installed as the new god. As the number of deceased bulls increased, the prince had a stairway cut into the Saqqara rock and added small burial vaults. Individual chapels were eventually done away with and one great stone shrine to Apis was erected. The prince endowed divine offerings and feasts to be held throughout the year, a tradition that lasted for thousands of years. In the New Kingdom, Apis carried the sun disk between his horns. From the late period on, he was depicted on coffins, carrying the mummy of the deceased, at a trot, to the grave. During the Greco-Roman period, the Apis cult grew in importance.

spirited and would be qualified for leadership. When Ramses was a boy, Sethos I had prescribed the same strenuous training for him.

One day, from the ancient Semitic city of Babylon, Ramses accepted a princess to his harem. This royal and simple gesture appeared to establish peaceful relations between the two countries. The generous gift, however, created jealousy with King Hattusil, who still simmered over the young Hittite prince's asylum in Egypt. Ramses appeared to be unconcerned.

CHANGES IN THE ROYAL FAMILY

In the twenty-fourth year of Ramses' reign, the two great temples at Abu Simbel in Nubia were completed—one for Ramses II and his gods, the other for Nefertari and her goddess. A giant statue of Ramses and a rounded figure of Queen Nefertari with smaller figures of their children flanked the sun-bleached portals. Ramses had hieroglyphics inscribed above the giant figures that read, "Rammesses II, he has made a Temple, excavated in the Mountain of eternal workmanship . . . for the Chief Queen Nefertari Beloved of Mut, in Nubia, forever and ever . . . Nefertari . . . for whose sake the very sun does shine!" according to Christian Jacq's *The Lady of Abu Simbel.*

A grand flotilla of royalty sailed up the Nile to Nubia. Ramses and Nefertari were accompanied by their daughter Princess Meritamun. But, in a rock stele, outside the temple, it portrayed only Ramses and Meritamun worshipping the gods. There was no record of the queen's participation. Had Nefertari not survived the long journey? Shortly after the inauguration, about 1255 b.c., we learned she had died.

Nefertari's monument revealed a splendor beyond all the others Ramses had built. Historian Bernadette Menu wrote that it was, "a masterpiece of Egyptian painting, richly decorated with mythological scenes. Gods and goddesses are depicted either alone or with the queen, who worships them or presents offerings to them. . . . The goddess Maat spreads her wings in protective gesture."

The royal custom of secession had changed with the death of Queen Nefertari. Assistant Queen Isetnofret became the great royal wife. Her first daughter, Bintanath, assumed her mother's previous role. Meritamun, Nefertari's eldest daughter, reigned as associate queen. Isetnofret's eldest son became heir apparent. Four daughters of Ramses also held the title of associate queen. These were the most exalted among his daughters, of whom there were at least 40 in addition to some 45 sons. Isetnofret bore Ramses' gifted son Merenptah, a famous magician who ultimately made the greatest mark in Egypt and attained kingship. Another son, Prince Khaemwaset, became the first Egyptologist, as he preserved the ancient monuments. He served as high priest of the god Ptah with a steady stream of high government positions.

With the turnaround in queenship, family matters were further complicated by the Hittites. King Hattusil now offered his daughter Maathorneferure to Ramses as first royal wife and royal queen. Queen Pudukhepa, Hattusil's wife, mapped out the rules of the royal marriage. She had to be assured her daughter would become the main queen in the harem. Despite Isetnofret's new royal crown, Ramses appeared to acknowledge Pudukhepa's wishes. "And you (gods) give her to the house of the king! And she will be the ruling (queen) of the Egyptians," wrote Dr. Sameh M. Arab. However, before final matrimonial agreements were completed, Queen Isetnofret died.

"When the daughter of the king of Hatti arrived in Egypt, soldiers, charioteers and dignitaries of His Majesty escorted her, mixing with soldiers and charioteers of Hatti, forming a single army composed of Asian and Egyptian soldiers; they ate and drank together, and like brothers they shared a single heart; no one rejected another, peace and brotherhood dwelt among

Ramses II outlived all of his sons born by Nefertari, and kingship was passed on to the children he shared with his second wife, Isetnofret. After his death, the thirteenth son of Ramses II, Merenptah *(above)* was named pharaoh of Egypt.

them according to the designs of god himself, the King of Upper and Lower Egypt, Usermaatre Setepenre, son of *Re*, Ramesses Beloved of Amun, blessed with Life," wrote Bernadette Menu. Ramses' marriage to the Hittite princess included a plentiful dowry. Ten years later, King Hattusil sent another daughter to join the royal harem.

In ancient times, pharaohs could have several wives but only one royal queen. The kings married their sisters and daughters, probably to reinforce their dynastic claim to the throne and to echo the behavior of the gods, who were believed to favor the practice. Of Ramses' seven royal wives, four were said to be his daughters.

Of Ramses many children, several sons became heir apparent. Over the 67 years of his long reign, with the dangers of warfare, untold diseases, and accidents, some died before him. All the sons of Queen Nefertari had died, and their legacy passed to the sons of Queen Isetnofret. When at last Ramses succumbed in 1212 B.C., it was his thirteenth son, Prince Merenptah by Isetnofret, who became the next pharaoh.

THE GREAT PHARAOH'S DEATH

In the year 1212 B.C., Ramses II joined the gods. He had lived 92 years in a land and time where life expectancy was half that. He had reigned for 67 years and lived to see all of his monuments completed, and the deaths of his beloved Nefertari, his youthful passion, Isetnofret, and his twelve oldest sons. His tomb had long been prepared in the Valley of the Kings, larger than that of his father, Sethos I. News of the great king's death passed rapidly throughout the land. Preparations for his burial had no sooner begun than a tremendous outpouring of grief spread across Egypt. After the 70 days of mourning and embalmment, his mummy was placed on the royal golden barge accompanied by the new pharaoh, Merenptah. One last time, Ramses II sailed past the ancient city of Memphis and beyond the fertile corridor of the upper Nile to his final resting place in the Valley of the Kings.

"The earthly cult of the dead king as a god was maintained in his memorial-temple 'of millions of years' . . . while his body slumbered in gold in the valley tomb and his spirit circled through day and night, night and day, as Osiris and Re, through nether world and heaven for ever," wrote Kenneth A. Kitchen.

Egypt
Thereafter

IN 1813, J. L. BURCKHARDT, PREPARING TO LEAVE EGYPT BY WAY OF THE
Nile, came upon the façade of a great temple. At Abu Simbel, buried under 11 centuries of Egyptian sand, Burckhardt
found two temples, those of Ramses II and his wife, Nefertari. Four years later, Giovanni Battista Belzoni, who stood
6 feet 7 inches and once worked in a sideshow demonstrat-
ing feats of strength, came to Egypt. Belzoni came to show
Pasha Mehemet Ali a hydraulic machine of his own invention
for raising the waters of the Nile. The pasha turned the idea
down. But, on the recommendation of Burckhardt, still travel-
ing in Egypt, Belzoni went to view the Ramesseum at Thebes.
There, he carefully removed the colossal bust of Ramses II,

commonly called "the Young Memnon," and shipped it to the British Museum in England, where it remains on prominent display.

Belzoni later explored the ruins of the great temple of Edfu and visited Elephantine and Philae. At Abu Simbel he cleared away years of sand and revealed the great temple. Two years later he made excavations at Karnak and opened the sepulcher of Sethos I (sometimes known as Belzoni's Tomb). The Italian explorer was the first to penetrate the second pyramid of Giza, and the first European in modern times to visit the oasis of Bahariya. In 1819 he returned to England and wrote an account of his travels called *Narrative of the Operations and Recent Discoveries Within the Pyramids, Temples, Tombs, and Excavations in Egypt and Nubia.*

Four years later he went to West Africa, intending to go to Timbuktu. Refused admission to Morocco, he instead traveled along the Guinea Coast. In Benin he was seized with dysentery and died. Celebrated traveler Richard Francis Burton contradicted this account and said Belzoni was murdered and robbed in West Africa. His cause of death remained in question but the magnificent Egyptian monuments became a "must see." Despite having to sail many miles on the Nile, face scorching desert heat, and trudge against blowing sand, Victorians were eager to visit the ancient tombs.

RAMSES JOINS THE GODS

The long reign of Ramses II was Egypt's last period of national grandeur. The number and size of the temples and tombs he built rivaled those of the Pyramid Age. He expanded international trade into the Mediterranean countries and east to Asia. Palace opulence exceeded that of all prior kings, and harmony lasted an entire empire. Kenneth A. Kitchen compared Ramses' kingship to that of Queen Victoria's Great Britain: "a reign that marked an epoch known for its great events and characteristic monumental style . . . stamped indelibly upon the nation's history in each case."

THE NEXT 3,000 YEARS

Sovereign rule gradually decayed as a succession of Ramses followed. Through the Twentieth Dynasty, ten pharaohs took his name. In 1191 B.C., Ramses III defeated the notorious Sea People from the Mediterranean islands, but after that, power within passed from the pharaohs to the priests of Amun.

For several centuries, Egypt was invaded and ruled by Islamic empires. A brief rule by Nubia occurred in the seventh and eighth centuries B.C. The Assyrians occupied Thebes in 666 B.C., while Psammetichus I restored Egypt's independence and unity. Eighty-four years later Egypt was conquered by Cambyses and became a province of Persia. Another period of independence followed. Alexander the Great added Egypt to his empire in 332 B.C. and appointed his general Ptolemy I, who founded the dynasty that ruled from Alexandria. These monarchs spoke Greek and worshiped Greek gods and goddesses, yet on temple walls they were portrayed as traditional Egyptian rulers. In about 30 B.C. Egypt passed into the hands of the Romans, and the emperors gradually followed the conversion to Christianity. Churches and monasteries replaced the temples. The version of Christianity that eventually triumphed was called Coptic. The Arab invasion of the seventh century A.D. turned Egypt into the mainly Muslim country that it is today. Sunni Islam is the chief religion. A small minority of Coptic Christians remain.

EGYPT AT THE CROSSROADS OF THREE CONTINENTS

Why were there so many conquerors and long and drawn-out campaigns fought over Egypt? The country lies in the strategic

The Temple of Amun of Luxor *(above)*, the statues at Abu Simbel, and other structures built during the reign of Ramses II continue to attract thousands of tourists
to Egypt every year. His creation of elaborate, jaw-dropping structures has made
Ramses II one of the most famous rulers in history.

corner of northeast Africa. It is bounded in the north by the
Mediterranean, the east by the Suez Canal and the Red Sea,
the south by Sudan, and the west by Libya. The vast Nile River
connects the Mediterranean Sea with nine African countries.
Egypt has an abundance of natural resources: iron ore, gold,
natural gas, phosphates, limestone, gypsum, talc, asbestos, lead,
zinc, and crude oil reserves. In 1869, the French completed the

Suez Canal, an artificial waterway 100 miles (160 km) long, running from Port Said to Suez. It linked the Mediterranean and Red seas, separated Africa from Asia, and provided the shortest eastward sea route from Europe. Nineteen years later, the Convention of Constantinople opened the Suez Canal to all nations. In 1914, Egypt became a British protectorate. Twenty-two years later, independence was achieved, and in 1953 Egypt was declared a republic.

The Rosetta Stone

Deciphering the Rosetta Stone was the key to understanding ancient Egypt, its laws and rulers, the people, the sacred gods, and the vast size of the empire itself. When the last temple was closed in the sixth century A.D., the skill of reading hieroglyphics was lost. In 1799, during Napoleon's campaign in Egypt, French engineer Captain Pierre-Francois Bouchard was guiding construction works near the Egyptian port city of Rosetta. There, he discovered a stone created in 196 B.C. On its face were three different scripts. The lowest portion was in Greek, the center in demotic (a cursive script for quick writing), the top in hieroglyphics. It weighed approximately 1,676 pounds and was originally thought to be granite or basalt. It is currently described as granodiorite and is dark-blue-pinkish-grey in color. Bouchard understood the stone's importance and showed it to General Jacques de Menou.

The stone was taken to France where French archaeologist Jean-Francois Champollion spent many years attempting to decipher its symbols. Fascinated with languages since a boy, Champollion learned 11 languages, including Greek and Hebrew. He found an Egyptian obelisk with cartouches that he believed held the names of Cleopatra and

THE ASWAN HIGH DAM

To guard against overflooding or drought, Ramses and his people prayed to the Nile god Hapi. Often their prayers were answered, and sometimes their fertile soil baked hard from a blazing sun and drought. In 1960, to keep the level of the Nile constant throughout the year without flooding, the mammoth Aswan Dam project began. Construction took 10 years, considerably less time than it took to build the pyramids or

the Greek ruler Ptolemy. He knew the Greeks had not forced their language upon their Egyptian subjects.

Champollion discovered that *Ptolemy* and *Cleopatra* had common letters. P was the first letter of one, and the fifth letter of the other—the first hieroglyphic sign was the same as the second one. From these identical letters, he learned 12 letters of the ancient Egyptian alphabet, but there were 24 letters in all. To complicate his work, there was sometimes only one single letter or a whole syllable or an unpronounced sign. The Egyptians had doubled up on their spelling. For the word *saw* they drew a picture of a saw. For *betray* a bee and a tray. Frustrated, Champollion nevertheless was not about to give up. Instead, he connected each of the signs with a sound instead of a picture. He recognized the name of Ptolemy on the Rosetta Stone and Cleopatra on a similar ancient monument.

In 1822, 23 years later, Champollion deciphered the full text. Today Champollion's work is considered an important breakthrough in the translation of ancient hieroglyphics. In 1801, the stone was captured by the British and placed in the British Museum in London. It left the museum only once. During World War II it was removed for safekeeping and stored in an English postal tube railway station 50 feet (15 m) below ground.

In 2003, the Egyptian government demanded the return of the Rosetta Stone. Two years later the British Museum sent a replica.

the Ramesseum. When the ancient temples were threatened by submersion in Lake Nasser because of the construction of the dam, the Egyptian government secured the support of UNESCO and launched a worldwide appeal. During the salvage operation, from 1964 through 1968, the two gigantic temples of Abu Simbel were dismantled and raised over 60 meters (196.8 ft) up the sandstone cliffs from where they had been built more than 3,000 years before. Here, they were reassembled in the exact relationship to each other and the sun and covered with an artificial mountain. Inside the temples it is still possible to see where the blocks were cut. The man-made dome is visible, and there is an exhibition of photographs showing the different stages of the massive removal project. Just think what Ramses II could have accomplished with modern technology.

RAMSES GOES TO PARIS

Ramses' original burial site in the Valley of the Kings became vulnerable to grave robbers. In 1871, the mummy was found in the great cache of royal mummies at the elegant mortuary temple of Deir el-Bahri. A script inside showed that the mummy had been removed from his previous resting place in the Twenty-first Dynasty to that of his father's, whence it was removed again to the museum in Thebes.

In 1976, the mummy of Ramses II was once again moved, making international headlines. Flown to Paris for a great Ramses II exhibition, the mummy was greeted at the airport by a full presidential guard of honor, much like a head of state would receive. At the museum experts noticed deterioration on the mummy, so it was examined by xeroradiography, and the best conservation treatment was performed. Afterward, Ramses II returned to Egypt. His mummy now resides in the Egyptian Museum in Cairo.

Long, long ago, Ramses the Great was proclaimed the living image of the sun god Re. While still a boy, he conformed to the laws of Maat, personified by justice, truth, and the proper order of life. His sacred baptism in the legend of Osiris became his bastion of Egyptian kingship. Early on, we learned he had excelled in mathematics, science, chemistry, and classical sports. Later as leader of all Egypt, he negotiated the first-ever peace treaty and ended long years of wars and hostilities with the Hittite. Two copies of the treaty survived, and a third hangs eminently at United Nations headquarters in New York City.

"Riding into battle with his pet lion often by his side, Ramses slew his enemies by the score and won heroic battles almost single-handedly—or at least that's the story he wanted to leave behind," wrote the editors of National Geographic in Treasures of Egypt. "The truth was more modest, but a modest man does not stud the landscape with dozens of colossal statues of himself." Nevertheless, "By the time of his death he had come to embody the power and magic of imperial Egypt so strongly that ten later kings adopted his name."

He played a key role as Egypt expanded and solidified against its various foes: the Libyans, Hittites, and Nubians. A powerful sovereign and great leader, Ramses was also a romantic who wrote endearing verse to his beloved great royal wife, Queen Nefertari. He delighted in her beauty and sought her intelligence and wisdom at court. He built her a magnificent sandstone tomb that was recently restored by an international team backed by the J. Paul Getty Museum in Los Angeles.

Commanding, driven to surpass all his predecessors, and charismatic, Ramses personified 67 years of peace and tranquility. His ancient kingdom endures today as a land of mystery and classical beauty, with exotic remnants of a long-ago past, enhanced and filtered with art and sculpture, temples and pyramids. Travelers from around the world still sail the Nile to visit his impressive legacies. They sleep in hotels named Ramses II, stroll boulevards called Ramses, and recline in Ramses parks. They visit Egyptian museums to view and study his ancient script and artifacts, and even his mummy. Thirty-five hundred years later, Ramses the Great is everywhere.

Bernadette Menu summed up the great pharaoh thusly: "It may truthfully be said that the reign of Ramessess II marked a point of culmination in pharaonic history. Under his administration the imperial power of Egypt grew immensely, and the empire greatly extended its international political authority and its cultural and religious influence."

CHRONOLOGY

◆ ◆ ◆

3100 B.C.	Late Predynastic period
3100	King Menes founds Memphis
2950	Early Dynastic period
2575	Old Kingdom; Pyramids and Sphinx are built
2125	First Intermediate period
2000–1800	Middle Kingdom
1630	Second Intermediate period
1539	New Kingdom
1301	Ramses' probable date of birth
1291	Ramses named commander in chief of Egyptian army
1290	Ramses named chief regent; likely date of marriage to Nefertari
1289	Ramses joins Sethos I in military campaign that captures Amurru and Qadesh
1287	Ramses participates in Sethos's Libyan campaign
1280	Prince regent takes part in Sherden Pirate (Sea People) campaign
1279	Death of King Sethos I
1279	Ramses is crowned king of Egypt

1277	Ramses begins construction of new capital Piramses and the Ramesseum
1274	Battle of Qadesh
1272	Approximate date of design of Abu Simbel
1259	Peace treaty with Hittites
1258	Death of Queen Tuya
1255	Dedication of Abu Simbel
1255	Death of Queen Nefertari
1254	Isetnofret is crowned great royal wife
1246	Approximate year of death of Queen Isetnofret
1246	Ramses marries Hittite princess Maathorneferure
1236	Ramses marries a second Hittite princess
1225	Ramses declares Merenptah as heir
1212	Ramses dies in August
1193	Fall of the Hittite Empire
1191	Ramses III defeats the Sea People
332	Alexander the Great founds Alexandria
304–285	Ptolemy I rules Egypt
51–48	Cleopatra rules Egypt
A.D. 1799	Napoleon's Egypt campaign
1799	Discovery of the Rosetta Stone
1822	Champollion deciphers the Rosetta Stone
1869	Completion of the Suez Canal
1813	J. L. Burckhardt unearths Abu Simbel
1953	Egypt becomes a republic
1960	Construction begins on Aswan Dam
1964	Abu Simbel dismantled and moved to higher ground
1976	Ramses' mummy goes to Paris museum

BIBLIOGRAPHY

◆ ◆ ◆

Alavosus, Laura, and John Bergez, eds. *History Alive*. Palo Alto, Calif: TCI, 2004.

Alderson, Brian, and Michael Foreman, illustrator. *The Arabian Nights*. New York: Morrow Junior Books, 1995.

Donoughue, Carol. *The Mystery of Hieroglyphs*. New York: University Press, 1999.

Gardiner, Alan, Sir. *The Kadesh Inscriptions of Ramesses II*. Oxford, England: Griffith Institute, 1960.

Grimal, Nicolas. *A History of Ancient Egypt*. Translated by Ian Shaw. London: Oxford University Press, 1988.

Grimal, Nicolas. *The Oxford History of Ancient Egypt*. Translated by Ian Shaw. London: Oxford University Press, 2000.

Hammond World Atlas Corp. *Hammond Compact Peters World Atlas*. Union, N.J.: Hammond World Atlas, 2002.

Harris, Geraldine. *Gods and Pharaohs*. New York: Peter Bedrick Books, 1981.

Heinrichs, Ann. *Egypt*. Rev. ed. New York: Children's Press, 2007.

Holmes, Burton. *Burton Holmes Travel Stories*. Chicago: Wheeler Publishing Company, 1931.

The Holy Bible. Revised Standard Edition. New York: T. Nelson, 1952.

Jacq, Christian. *The Eternal Temple.* Translated by Mary Feeney. New York: Warner Books, 1998.

Jacq, Christian. *The Lady of Abu Simbel.* Translated by Mary Feeney. New York: Warner Books, 1998.

Jacq, Christian. *The Son of Light.* Translated by Mary Feeney. New York: Warner Books, 1997.

Kitchen, Kenneth A. *Pharaoh Triumphant: The Life and Times of Ramses II.* Warminster, England: Aris & Phillips Ltd., 1982.

Lichtheim, Miriam. *Ancient Egyptian Literature, Vol II.* Berkeley, Calif.: University of California Press, 1976.

Menu, Bernadette. *Ramessess II: Greatest of the Pharaohs.* New York: Harry N. Abrams, Inc., 1999.

Mintz, Barbara. *Hieroglyphs: the Writing of Ancient Egypt.* New York: Margaret K. McElderry Books, 1981.

Pateman, Robert, and Salwa El-Hamamsy. *Egypt.* 2nd ed. New York: Benchmark Books, 2004.

Payne, Elizabeth. *The Pharaohs of Ancient Egypt.* New York: Random House, 1964.

Reader's Digest. *Magic and Medicine of Plants.* New York: Reader's Digest Association, 1986.

Romer, John. *Ancient Lives: Daily Life in Egypt of the Pharaohs.* New York: Holt, Rinehart, and Winston, 1984.

Shaw, Ian. *The Oxford History of Ancient Egypt.* Revised ed. London: Oxford University Press, 2000.

Unger, Merrill F. *The New Unger's Bible Dictionary.* Chicago: Moody Press, 1988.

Webster's New World Encyclopedia. New York: Prentice Hall, 1992.

Whiting, Jim. *The Life and Times of Rameses the Great.* Hockessin, Del.: Mitchell Lane Publishers, 2005.

WEB SITES

www.ancientegypt.org

classics.mit.edu/Herodotus/history.2.ii.html

www.history-world.org/osiris_and_the_history_of_abydos.htm

www.nefertit.iwebland.com

www.touregypt.net/PreceptsofPtahhotep.htm

FURTHER READING

◆ ◆ ◆

Clayton, Peter A. *Chronicle of the Pharaohs*. London: Thames & Hudson, 1994.

Halliwell, Sarah. *Gods and Pharaohs of Ancient Egypt*. Edison, N.J.: Chartwell Books, 1998.

Hart, George. *Ancient Egypt*. London: DK Publishing, Inc., 2004.

Menu, Bernadette. *Ramessess II: Greatest of the Pharaohs*. New York: Harry N. Abrams, Inc., 1999.

Payne, Elizabeth. *The Pharaohs of Ancient Egypt*. New York: Random House, 1964.

Whiting, Jim. *The Life and Times of Rameses the Great*. Hockessin, Del.: Mitchell Lane Publishers, 2005.

WEB SITES

www.ancientegypt.org

www.history-world.org.

www.touregypt.net

PHOTO CREDITS

◆ ◆ ◆

page:

Frontis: ©Erich Lessing / Art
Resource, NY
14: © Scala/ Art Resource, NY
21: © DeA Picture Library/
Art Resource, NY
26: ©Werner Forman / Art
Resource, NY
32: © Vanni / Art Resource, NY
38: © Bridgeman-Giraudon /
Art Resource, NY
43: © Nimatallah / Art
Resource, NY
48: © Werner Forman / Art
Resource, NY
56: © British Museum/ Art
Resource, NY
62: © Vanni/ Art Resource, NY

67: © Scala/ Art Resource,
NY
73: © Erich Lessing / Art
Resource, NY
79: © Erich Lessing / Art
Resource, NY
85: © Vanni / Art Resource, NY
94: © Erich Lessing / Art
Resource, NY
98: © Gianni Dagli Orti/
CORBIS
103: © Erich Lessing / Art
Resource, NY
107: © Werner Forman / Art
Resource, NY
113: © François Guenet / Art
Resource, NY

INDEX

◆ ◆ ◆

A

Abu Simbel temples, 16–17, 34, 60, 71, 88–89, 105, 110–111, 116
Abydos, 25–26, 35, 42–43, 59, 65–66
Aha (King), 25–26, 65–66
Ahmose II, 84, 96
Akkadian, 92
Aksha, 61
Albert, Lake, 49
Alexander the Great, 112
Ali, Mehemet, 110–111
Amen-em-inet, 36
Amenhikhopeshef (Prince), 68
Amenotep III, 55
Amorites, 51
amulets, 41, 47, 104
Amun, 55, 75, 78
Amunherwenemef, 38–39
Amun-Re, 54–55, 57, 60, 71
Amurru, 33, 74–75, 92
antibiotics, 84
Anubis, 27, 43, 68
Apiru, 52–54, 96
Apis (god), 19, 87, 104
Arabian Eastern Desert, 49
arrows, 77
Asha-hebsed, 36
Aswan, 37
Aswan Dam, 115–116

Atbara, 49
Avaris, 41, 69

B

baptism, 42–44, 117
Bast, 87
Beautiful Feast of the Nile Valley, 59
Bedouins, 51
Beit el-Wali, 39
Beithetepe, 28
Belzoni, Giovanni Battista, 110–111
Benteshina (Hittite Prince), 74–75
Berenib (Queen), 28
Bers, Georg, 83
Bintanath (Queen), 68, 106
Blue Nile, 49
Book of the Dead, 17, 20, 68, 88
Bouchard, Pierre-Francois, 114
Brest-Litovsk, Treaty of, 95
bulls, 19, 87, 104. *See also* Apis
Burckhardt, J.L., 110–111
Burton, Richard Francis, 111

C

Caesar, Augustus, 28
calendars, 54, 58

Cambyses, 112
Capture of Joppa, 65
cemetery, crocodile, 32–33
challenges, 13–15, 21–22,
    43–44
Champollion, Jean-François,
    114–115
chariots, 76, 101
Cheops, 29, 63
children of Ramses the Great,
    17, 37–39, 88, 108. *See also*
    Isnetofret
Christianity, 112
coffins, 41
Confucianism, 20
coronations, 27, 44–45, 57
courage, 13–15, 21–22, 43–44
crocodiles, 32–33, 87
cuneiform, 92
Cyrus (King of Persia), 84

D

daggers, 77
Damietta, 49
death of Ramses the Great,
    108–109
Deir el-Bahri, 69, 116
Deir el-Medina, 61
Deniu-en-Khons, 87
dill, 84
diseases, 86–87
Djer, 28
Djoser (King), 29

E

Edfu, 111
education, 13, 59
Edwin Smith Papyrus, 84
Egypt, location of, 46–47,
    112–114
embalming process, 40–41
Exodus, 96–97
extradition clauses, 92

F

Faiyum, 32
falcon kings, 25
farming, Nile River and, 24
Fellahin, 50
First Intermediate Period, 31
flax, 85
flooding, 18, 24, 48, 115
flowers, 52–53, 55, 72
Foredoomed Prince, The, 65

G

Gallery of Lists, 42
games, 64–65
garlic bulbs, 84
General Sisenet, 65
Ghost Story, 65
Gift of the Nile, 46
Giza, 29, 31, 63
gods. *See also specific gods*
    Abu Simbel Temple and, 71
    armies and, 75
    baptism and, 43–44
    flowers and, 52–53, 55
    kings as, 27
    overview of, 25, 27–28
    peace treaty and, 92
    words of, 17
gold, 74, 82, 113
Golden Age, 33, 104
Great Pyramid at Giza, 29, 63
Great Temple of Ramses II, 88

H

Ham, 50
Hamites, 50–54
Hanigalbat, 89
Hapi, 74, 115
Hardjedef, 65
Harsomtus, 52
Hathor, 68, 87, 88
Hatshepsut (Queen), 69

Hattusil (Hittite King), 89–90, 92, 100, 105
Hebrews, 53–54
Hentmire (sister), 102
Hequet, 87
Herodotus, 29, 31
hieroglyphics, 13, 16–17, 30, 41, 114–115
Hittite Empire, 12–13, 18, 33, 59, 72–82, 89–94, 106–108
Homer, 83–84
Horemheb, 39
horses, 101
Horus, 25, 43, 52, 86, 87
human sacrifices, 65–66
Hurrians, 51
Hypostyle Hall of Columns, 61, 88

I

Iat-Rek, 47
Imhotep, 29, 65, 83
immortality, 32
Isabella (Queen of Spain), 99
Isetnofret (daughter), 34, 37, 68, 72, 106
Isis, 27

J

Jacob, 53
John II (King of Portugal), 99
Joseph, 53

K

Ka, 25, 41
Kagera River, 49
Karnak, 44, 59, 61, 88, 92, 111
Khaemwaset, 38–39, 106
Khnum, 87
Khufu (Pharaoh), 29, 63
kings as gods, 27
Knons, 55
Kyoga, Lake, 49

L

League of Nations, 95
Leiden Papyrus, 96
Libya, 18, 33, 59
lions, 18, 80
lotus flowers, 52, 72
Luxor, 57, 61

M

Maat, 19–20, 27, 42, 44, 59, 71, 102, 117
magic, 16–17
marble quarry, 37
medicine, 83–87
Medina, 61–63
Medinet el-Ghurob, 96
Memphis, 18–19, 25–26
Menes (King), 18–19, 28, 49
Menou, Jacques de, 114
Merenptah (King), 108
meridians, 97, 99
Meritamun (Queen), 68, 106
Middle Kingdom, 31–33
Mnevis, 87, 104
Moses, 19, 96–97
Mound of Creation, 55
mummies, 29, 32, 40–42, 69, 104, 116–117
music, 24, 64–65
Muslim faith, 112
mustard, 84
Mut, 55
Mutwatallis (Hittite King), 33, 75–80
Myth of the Eye and the Sun, 65

N

Narmer, 25
Nasser, Lake, 49, 116
natron, 40
Nebettawy, 68
Neb-iot, 60

Nefertari (Queen), 34, 37, 42, 45, 67–68, 71, 92–94, 102, 105–106
Nerberry, Percy, 52–53
New Kingdom, 33, 104
Nile River Valley, 23–25, 46–49, 113–116
Nilometer, 47–49
Nubia, 28, 37–39, 51, 59, 61, 74

O

obelisks, 61
Old Kingdom, 28–31
Opening of the Mouth, 41
Opet Festival, 54–57
orchards, 52–53
Orontes River, 77
Osiris, 27–28, 39–44, 59, 68, 88, 117
Osiris temple, 37
Ozymandias (Shelley), 80–81

P

papyrus, 30, 52, 65, 83–85, 96
Papyrus Ebers, 58, 83
Papyrus Harris I, 96
Paris, Treaty of, 95
Paser, 60
peace treaties, 18, 89, 91–99, 117
Pepi I, 47
Petrie, Flinders, 52–53
Piramses, 41, 69–70, 72
pirates, 39
Pliny the Elder, 52
pomegranates, 53
Portugal, 99
priests, 30, 86–87, 101
prince regent title, 36
Psammetichus I, 112
Ptah, 19, 71, 75, 87, 104, 106
Ptahhotep, Vizier, 20
Ptolemy, 115
Pudukhepa, 92, 106–108

Pyramid Age, 28–31, 110–111
pyramids, 28–31

Q

Qadesh, 18, 33, 75–81, 82, 92
Qantir, 69–70
quarries, 37

R

Ra Harakhi, 71
Ramesseum, 61, 80, 92
Ramses III, 112
Rawdah, 48
Re, 25, 27, 69, 75
Red Land, 49
Rekhmira, 101
resin, 41
rituals, 86–87
Roman Empire, 112
rosemary, 84
Rosetta Stone, 17, 114–115
Rosette, 49

S

sacrifices, human, 65–66
Sahara Desert, 49–50
Saqqara, 19, 29, 104
sarcophagus, 41, 68
scales, 40
scribes, 30, 33–34, 54
Sea People (Sheriden pirates), 39, 59, 112
Second Pyramid of Giza, 31
Sed Festival, 102
sekhem, 58–59
Seth, 27, 75
Sethos I (father), 12–15, 27, 35–36, 59, 111
Seven Wonders of the World, 29
Shelley, Percy Bysshe, 80–81
Sherden pirates (Sea People), 39, 59, 112

shields, 76–77
Sinai Peninsula, 50
Sirius, 58
Sixth Dynasty, 19
slavery, 51–52, 59, 63
Snake (game), 65
Snofu (King), 29
Sobek, 27, 32–33, 87
social position, 54
songs, 24, 64–65
Sothic date, 58
Spain, 99
Sphinx, 31
spiritual baptism, 42–44, 117
Step Pyramid, 29
stone workers, 22, 61–63
Suez Canal, 114
sun god, 25, 27, 69, 75
surgery, 84

T

Table of Abydos, 59
Tale of Two Brothers, 65
Ta-Set-Neferu, 68
taxes, 60
Tell Nabi Mend. *See* Qadesh
temples. *See also* Abu Simbel
   temples
      of Abydos, 35
      Battle of Qadesh and, 80
      at Beit el-Wali, 39
      at Karnak, 44, 59
      Osiris, 37, 59
      repair of, 66
Thebes, 37, 60, 61
Thoth, 17, 87

Thutmose I (King), 69
Thutmose III, 69
Tia (sister), 13, 102
tombs, 17, 25–26. *See also specific tombs*; Valley of the Kings;
   Valley of the Queens
Tordesillas, Treaty of, 97, 99
treaties, 18, 89, 91–99, 117
Tunip, 82
Turquoise City, 72
Tuthmose III, 96
Tuya (mother), 13, 42, 72, 102
Twentieth Dynasty, 112
Tyra, 74

U

Urhi-Teshub (Hittite King), 89, 100
Usi-am-re, 36, 81

V

Valley of the Kings, 41–42, 61, 63–64, 68–69, 108–109, 116
Valley of the Queens, 66–68, 88, 102
Versailles, Treaty of, 95
Victoria, Lake, 49
viziers, 20, 60

W

wadis, 49, 59, 74
weapons, 76–77
White Nile, 49
workers' village, 61

ABOUT THE AUTHORS

◆ ◆ ◆

SILVIA ANNE SHEAFER is a teacher and a national awarding-winning author, journalist, and photographer. She is editor of the *International Senior Traveler* and travels frequently, writing magazine and newspaper travel articles.

ARTHUR SCHLESINGER, JR. is remembered as the leading American historian of our time. He won the Pulitzer Prize for his books *The Age of Jackson* (1945) and *A Thousand Days* (1965), which also won the National Book Award. Schlesinger was the Albert Schweitzer Professor of the Humanities at the City University of New York and was involved in several other Chelsea House projects, including the series *Revolutionary War Leaders*, *Colonial Leaders*, and *Your Government*.